TEAMS THAT BUILDS THE KINGDOM

SERVING THE APOSTOLIC VISION

TOM CORNELL

SOZO PUBLISHING

CONTENTS

Introduction   vii

1. The Set Man and the Apostolic Blueprint   1
2. The Nature of Apostolic Covering   8
3. Apostolic Culture   17
4. From Crowd to Core   25
5. How to Catch the Spirit of Your Leader   32
6. The Power of Submission and Alignment   40
7. Stages of Maturity in an Apostolic House   49
8. Why You're Not Given Too Much Too Soon   57
9. From Helper to Steward — Growing in
   Responsibility   65
10. The Apostolic Team   73
11. Communication, Correction, and Covenant   80
12. Guarding the House — Loyalty, Honor, and
    Warfare   87
13. Sons, Not Slaves — Serving from Inheritance,
    Not Obligation   95
14. Reproducing the Culture — From Disciple to
    Leader   102

Conclusion   109
About the Author   113

INTRODUCTION
WHY THE APOSTOLIC TEAM MATTERS

The Church was never meant to be a crowd gathered around a sermon. It was always meant to be a family built around a sent one.

From the beginning, God has advanced His Kingdom through divine order—by choosing, commissioning, and anointing specific leaders to carry His vision and raise up teams that would build what heaven has blueprint. In every generation, God sets a man—an apostolic leader—not to be worshiped, but to be followed, not to be idolized, but to be imitated, because he carries something from heaven that must be multiplied in the earth. And those who are called to that leader, that house, and that vision are not just members—they are builders, sons, and partners in destiny.

This book is written for you, the disciple who senses a call to build something bigger than yourself. You may be in a season where God is aligning you with an apostolic house, drawing you into deeper relationship with your leaders, and inviting you to serve a vision that wasn't born in your heart—

but will one day birth your calling. You are not just here to attend church. You are being positioned by God to help build His Kingdom through spiritual family, servant-hearted obedience, and maturing alignment.

From Attending to Building

There's a vast difference between those who attend a church and those who build a house. The attendees look for comfort; the builders look for assignment. Attendees come to receive; builders come to release. Attendees come when it's convenient; builders show up because they carry the burden of the house. God is shifting His people from passivity to participation. From membership to maturity. From being loosely connected to being deeply rooted.

The apostolic Church isn't a personality-driven event. It's a covenant community with a Kingdom purpose. And in apostolic houses, God is restoring the blueprint of the early church —not a man-made institution, but a Spirit-led family, governed by grace and truth, ordered by spiritual authority, and built by teams of maturing sons and daughters who know how to labor, serve, suffer, sacrifice, and steward the weight of God's assignment together.

Why the Team Matters

God never intended for apostles to carry the weight of vision alone. Every apostolic leader needs a team—an apostolic people—who don't just echo his words but carry his spirit. This is not about elitism. This is about order. This is not about favoritism. This is about function. Kingdom vision requires Kingdom alignment. And God always places people in houses —not randomly, but intentionally—to walk under covering, to be fathered into maturity, and to be trained, equipped, and released into their purpose through submission and service.

When Jesus chose His disciples, He didn't just give them assignments; He gave them access. He let them see His prayer life, His tears, His frustrations, His hunger, His glory. Why? Because team members aren't just co-laborers—they are carriers of DNA. Apostolic teams don't just fulfill tasks—they extend legacy. And to be part of such a team is both a high calling and a holy responsibility.

The Safety of Alignment

Many want the mantle without the maturity. They crave the microphone without the process. But in God's house, promotion flows through submission. Responsibility is given according to maturity. And alignment is not restriction—it's protection. Apostolic leaders are entrusted with the weight of stewarding not just gifts, but souls. That's why they don't release people too quickly or assign weight that character cannot yet carry. It's not to control. It's to preserve.

This book will challenge you to embrace the pace of your process, to understand the stages of your growth, and to submit to the order God has placed over your life. Because true spiritual authority doesn't come from self-appointment or ambition —it flows from being rightly aligned, fully submitted, and wholly yielded.

Catching the Spirit of Your Leader

It's one thing to admire your apostolic leader's teaching. It's another to catch their heart. Those who truly walk with their leader carry what he carries. They don't need titles to function or platforms to serve. They lead through loyalty, they build through burden, and they serve with spiritual eyes fixed on the bigger picture.

Elisha didn't receive Elijah's mantle by watching from afar —he stayed close, served well, and refused to leave. He caught his leader's spirit before he ever caught his power. Today, many want the power of their apostolic leader without catching the posture. But the apostolic team is not built through gifting alone—it's built through alignment, honor, covenant, and submission.

You don't become part of an apostolic team by networking. You become part of it by surrender.

This Book Is For...

This book is for every disciple who is tired of casual Christianity and senses the call to build.

This book is for every person who loves their apostolic leader but has questions about how to walk more fully in alignment and authority.

This book is for every believer who wants to mature, submit, and serve in a way that multiplies the Kingdom of God through spiritual family.

If you've ever asked:

- "How do I find my place in the vision of this house?"
- "How do I serve my apostolic leader well?"
- "Why haven't I been released into leadership yet?"

- "What does it really mean to walk as a son in the house?"
- "How do I catch the culture and heart of my spiritual family?"

...then this book is for you.

You will discover what God is doing through apostles today, why spiritual order matters, how to mature through the stages of responsibility, and how to go from just showing up to truly being set into the house to build. You'll also learn how to steward correction, grow in trust, and guard unity within the team. And ultimately, you will see the beauty of being part of something bigger than yourself—a Kingdom family that's advancing God's will on earth as it is in heaven.

So let's begin. Let the Holy Spirit speak to your heart. Let the Spirit of sonship rise in you. And let's build together.

CHAPTER 1
THE SET MAN AND THE APOSTOLIC BLUEPRINT

The Kingdom of God does not advance randomly. It advances through divine strategy, spiritual order, and appointed leadership. God does not build ministries around talents or popularity—He builds around vision. And every God-given vision comes with a God-appointed vessel. That vessel is what Scripture calls the set man—a leader divinely chosen, anointed, and sent to establish God's will in a region, through a people, and for a purpose.

In every generation, God raises up set men—apostolic leaders with a unique assignment to birth, establish, and expand Kingdom outposts in the earth. These men don't simply gather crowds or build events; they carry blueprints from Heaven to construct spiritual families, regional hubs, and governmental expressions of the Kingdom. And God calls others—not to replace the set man, but to walk with him, serve the vision, and carry the burden so the house can be built according to Heaven's pattern.

God Always Starts with a Man

When God wanted to build something new in the earth, He didn't start with a committee—He started with a man.

- He called Noah to build an ark before there was a flood.
- He called Abraham to become a nation before there was even a child.
- He called Moses to lead a people before Pharaoh ever said yes.
- He called David to rule a kingdom before the throne was vacant.
- He called Paul to build churches in cities still full of idols.

God calls a man. Then He gives him a word. And that word becomes a blueprint.

The set man is not better than others, but he is chosen for a specific purpose. The oil that flows from his head is not about ego—it's about order (Psalm 133). Heaven honors the man that Heaven sends. And when people honor that order, they step into the flow of God's blessing, protection, and assignment.

The Blueprint is From Heaven

Apostles don't build based on preference—they build based on pattern. They carry a divine architecture for what the house should look like. Just like Moses was told, "See that you make everything according to the pattern shown to you on the mountain" (Hebrews 8:5*), every apostolic leader has a blueprint in the Spirit for how the house should function, grow, govern, and impact.

---

* ESV

This blueprint governs:

- How the culture is shaped
- How leaders are raised
- How vision is advanced
- How people are protected
- How the Kingdom is expressed

Apostles don't just preach sermons; they govern movements. They don't just build ministries—they birth spiritual families aligned with Heaven's government. And anyone called to be part of that family must understand the blueprint so they can build with precision, not presumption.

You don't build a roof when the foundation hasn't been laid. You don't start framing walls without understanding the structure. And you don't start a new ministry within a house unless you've been faithful to help build the house you were planted in.

The Weight of the Set Man's Assignment

The set man carries the weight of the vision. Not just the day-to-day tasks—but the burden of what God has called him to do. That burden includes revelation, responsibility, warfare, and accountability before God. He must hear clearly, move carefully, and build accurately.

Many admire the anointing but underestimate the weight. Many want the mantle but don't understand the cost. The set man may be gifted, but he is also wounded—wounded in obedience, misunderstood in assignment, and often walking alone in the Spirit long before others catch up to what God has shown him.

To be joined to such a man is not a light thing. It's not about favoritism or status. It's about covenant. God joins people to leaders in order to fulfill divine purpose. And your alignment to that set man can unlock dimensions of grace, maturity, and destiny in your life that cannot be accessed apart from God-ordained order.

Set Into the House, Not Just Around the House

Psalm 92:13 says, "Those who are planted in the house of the Lord shall flourish." NKJV

Notice—it does not say "those who attend the house." Planted means positioned. It implies roots, responsibility, and submission to the process.

In every apostolic house, people must move from watching the set man to catching the spirit of the set man. They must move from proximity to participation. From curiosity to covenant.

Being set in a house means:

- You're not here to shop for better soil.
- You're not comparing leaders.
- You're not questioning the architecture.

You're here to build what was shown—not to insert your own blueprint.

There is no greater honor than to be set by God into a house where Heaven's blueprint is being established. And the sooner you recognize your place in that vision, the sooner you can start helping to build what God has assigned to that leader.

You Don't Choose the Vision—You Catch It

Spiritual sons and daughters don't create the blueprint—they catch it. The apostolic leader is entrusted with the divine pattern, and those called to walk with him are not there to modify it, but to multiply it.

This is where many struggle. They want to influence the vision before they've served it. They want to shape the culture before they've been shaped by it. But Kingdom order says: first catch it, then carry it; first serve it, then steward it.

Elisha didn't demand his own school of prophets. He served Elijah faithfully, catching the vision, the spirit, and the burden of his leader. And because he submitted to the process, the mantle found him when the time came.

You don't carry authority in an apostolic house because of how gifted you are. You carry authority because of how aligned you are.

If the Set Man Is the Architect, You Are a Builder

Paul said in 1 Corinthians 3:10*, "As a wise master builder, I have laid the foundation, and another builds on it." Apostolic leaders are master builders. But they're not supposed to build alone. God gives them teams—sons and daughters, elders and deacons, ministers and helpers—who build with them, not just for them.

Your job is to become a wise builder. To understand the

---

* NKJV

blueprint. To learn the materials. To trust the architect. And to build what's been revealed.

It takes humility to build something you didn't design. But when you do, you become part of a legacy that will last longer than you.

Responding to the Blueprint

As you begin this journey of understanding the apostolic house, let this first truth settle deep in your spirit:

God sets a man before He sets a people. And if He's called you to the house, then He's called you to that man's vision. Not to critique it. Not to casually attend it. But to carry it—with passion, with purity, and with perseverance.

This is not about man-worship. It's about honoring God's divine order. It's not about losing your identity. It's about discovering your place. Because when you align with a God-ordained leader, you tap into a grace that matures you, equips you, and sends you into purpose.

So, who is the set man God has placed in your life?
What vision has he been entrusted to carry?
And how will you respond to that blueprint?

The answer to those questions could define your spiritual trajectory for decades to come.

Discussion Questions

1. **Divine Order and Alignment:** The chapter emphasizes that God builds around *vision*, not popularity, and that the "set man" carries Heaven's blueprint for a house or region. How does this challenge modern ideas of leadership and ministry? In what ways might honoring divine order bring greater fruitfulness to your life or church?

2. **Catching the Vision, Not Creating It:** The text says, *"You don't choose the vision—you catch it."* What does it practically look like to "catch" the spirit of your leader and build faithfully with someone else's vision? What heart posture is required to do this well?

3. **Building With Humility:** Paul described himself as a "wise master builder," but he also depended on others to build with him. Where is God calling you to build under someone else's blueprint right now—and what might need to shift in your mindset or habits so you can build with humility, unity, and faithfulness?

CHAPTER 2

THE NATURE OF APOSTOLIC COVERING

Covering is one of the most misunderstood concepts in the modern church. To some, it sounds restrictive. To others, unnecessary. For those who have been abused by controlling leaders, the idea of spiritual covering can feel like a threat to their freedom or personal relationship with God. But covering, in its biblical and apostolic form, is not control—it's protection. It is a divine structure that allows you to flourish in purpose without being exposed to spiritual danger.

Every Kingdom house must be covered. Every disciple must be planted under spiritual authority. Every team must operate under the shadow of governmental grace. Why? Because covering provides three essential realities: alignment, account-ability, and access.

And none of these are possible without the right heart posture.

What Is Apostolic Covering?

Apostolic covering is God's design to protect, position, and mature believers through spiritual family and appointed leadership. It's the structure that ensures God's authority flows in order. It is not about controlling lives—it's about cultivating destiny through relationship and submission to God's delegated authority.

A covering is a place of:

- Safety from deception
- Protection from demonic attack
- Correction when off-course
- Impartation for maturity and mission

Think of covering like a roof. It does not limit the size of the house—it protects it. It does not suppress what's inside—it shields what's valuable. And just like a roof must be properly connected to the walls to serve its purpose, a disciple must be connected to their apostolic leader—not just in name, but in spirit and posture.

Biblical Foundations of Covering

We see covering modeled from Genesis to Revelation.

- In the Garden, God was Adam's direct covering. When Adam rejected that covering through disobedience, he was exposed, vulnerable, and displaced.
- In Exodus, Moses was a covering for Israel. When the people rejected him, they opened themselves to judgment and delay.
- In the Gospels, Jesus covered His disciples. He prayed for them, protected them, and prepared them. They were safe under His leadership—even when they were immature.

- In Acts, Paul covered the churches he planted. He didn't just visit occasionally—he fathered them, warned them of wolves, and appointed elders to maintain the covering in his absence.

In each case, covering wasn't just functional—it was relational. It wasn't just authority—it was family. God's covering operates through spiritual fathers and apostolic leaders who have been set to govern, guide, and guard God's people with love, truth, and boldness.

What Covering Is Not

To appreciate true covering, we must first dismantle false definitions. Apostolic covering is not:

- Micromanagement: A true covering does not control every detail of your life. It equips you to make wise decisions with accountability and discernment.
- Hierarchy for status: Covering is not about position —it's about posture. It's not about who's on top—it's about who's under the weight of responsibility.
- Spiritual abuse: True apostles build people up, not tear them down. They bring correction in love, not with manipulation or fear.
- A license to bypass intimacy with God: Your relationship with your covering is never a substitute for your personal relationship with the Father. It should enhance your walk with God, not replace it.

If you've experienced a counterfeit version of covering, don't throw out the principle—restore the pattern.

The Blessing of Being Covered

There is great blessing in being under apostolic covering. Psalm 91 declares, "He who dwells in the secret place of the Most High shall abide under the shadow of the Almighty.*" When you abide under divine order, you are hidden, protected, and empowered to thrive.

Here's what covering provides:

1. Spiritual Protection — Your leader sees what you may not. Their prayers cover you. Their warnings guard you.
2. Impartation of Grace — What flows from the head flows to the body (Psalm 133). Alignment brings access to the anointing.
3. Correction in Love — Sons are corrected because they are loved. Orphans run from correction. Mature sons receive it with joy.
4. Commissioning for Assignment — Apostolic covering is where you are launched, not just affirmed. True covering sends you when the time is right.
5. Healing from Wounds — Many believers carry wounds from broken families and churches. Apostolic houses become places of reparenting—restoring trust and identity.

Covering doesn't crush you. It carries you. It's not a ceiling —it's a canopy of grace where you grow tall, strong, and safe.

Submitting to Covering Requires Humility

To come under covering, you must first come under. This is why submission is so resisted in our culture—it requires humil-

---

* NKJV

It requires dying to the pride that says, "I don't need anyone over me." But the truth is, everyone is under someone in God's Kingdom.

Jesus Himself was under the Father's covering. He said, "I only do what I see the Father doing"*. He didn't act independently, even though He had all power. If Jesus walked in submission, how much more should we?

Submission is not a sign of weakness—it is the gateway to spiritual authority. You cannot operate in Kingdom authority if you are not first under Kingdom authority.

And the proof of submission is not in your words—it's in your posture when you're corrected, challenged, or told to wait.

Covering Positions You for Responsibility

One of the primary functions of apostolic covering is to position you for responsibility—not just to keep you safe, but to prepare you to carry weight. Apostolic leaders are responsible for raising up builders, not just believers. And part of that process includes:

- Teaching you the culture of the house
- Watching how you respond to instruction
- Entrusting you with small assignments to test faithfulness
- Correcting areas of immaturity and helping you grow
- Releasing you at the right time with full support

---

* Paraphrase John 5:19

The goal of covering is not to hold you back, but to prepare you for sending.

Covering Requires Covenant, Not Convenience

In the world, relationships are based on convenience. But in the Kingdom, covering is based on covenant. That means you don't walk away when it's hard. You don't change churches because you were corrected. You don't abandon the house when your season of hiddenness feels long.

Covenant says:

- "I'm here because God planted me here."
- "I trust the vision and the leader God has given me."
- "Even when I don't understand, I remain submitted."
- "Correction is not rejection—it's love."

Apostolic covering thrives where there is covenant, not consumerism. The mature know that their destiny is tied to their alignment.

The Cost of Being Uncovered

To reject covering is to invite chaos. Many believers today function as spiritual freelancers—gifted, anointed, but uncovered. And the results are devastating: burnout, deception, moral failure, and isolation. When you are uncovered, you may move fast, but you won't move far.

The enemy's strategy is always to isolate you from your covering. He knows that when sheep wander from the shepherd, they become vulnerable prey. But when you remain under covering, you walk in the strength of a house, not just your own strength.

Jude 1:6 speaks of angels who "abandoned their proper dwelling." They left their rank, and as a result, they fell. In the same way, believers who leave their God-given covering often fall—not because they weren't gifted, but because they broke divine protocol.

Don't mistake exposure for elevation. Just because you can go doesn't mean you're sent. And just because something grows doesn't mean it has God's blessing. Only what's built in alignment with covering will remain.

Let Covering Be Your Catalyst

If you've struggled with the idea of covering, ask the Lord to renew your mind. Let Him show you the beauty, safety, and power of apostolic order. Covering is not a barrier—it's a bridge into maturity, responsibility, and destiny.

To walk in the fullness of your calling, you need more than gifting—you need alignment.

To be trusted with spiritual authority, you must first come under spiritual authority. To build something that lasts, you must be covered as you build. And when you come under covering with the right heart, you'll discover something powerful:

You are not losing freedom—you are gaining grace.

You are not shrinking—you are being shielded and strengthened for what's next.

You are not being held back—you are being held safe until the day of release.

So stay planted. Stay submitted. Stay covered. Because only covered sons become trustworthy builders.

Discussion Questions

1. **Redefining Covering:** The chapter describes covering not as *control* but as *protection*. How does this redefine your understanding of spiritual authority? Can you identify areas in your life where a right understanding of covering could bring healing or safety instead of restriction?

2. **Covenant vs. Convenience:** The text says, *"Apostolic covering thrives where there is covenant, not consumerism."* What's the difference between being part of a house out of covenant versus convenience? How can you cultivate a covenant heart even when seasons of correction or waiting feel uncomfortable?

3. **The Posture of Submission:** It says, *"The proof of submission is not in your words—it's in your posture when you're corrected, challenged, or told to wait."* Reflect on how you personally respond to correction or authority. What might God be teaching you about humility, trust, and spiritual maturity through your current leaders?

CHAPTER 3

APOSTOLIC CULTURE
BUILDING A KINGDOM FAMILY

Culture is more than what a house does—it's who the house is. In apostolic houses, culture isn't created by accident. It is built with intentionality. It is established through repetition. It is carried by sons and daughters. And it is guarded by those who understand its value.

Apostles don't just build churches—they establish Kingdom culture. That means that the apostolic house becomes more than a building or a Sunday service. It becomes a spiritual family, a governing hub, and an atmosphere where Heaven's values become the people's values.

And if you're called to be a builder in the house, then catching the culture of the house is not optional—it is essential.

What Is Apostolic Culture?

Culture is the invisible current that shapes everything. It's the way people think, speak, relate, and respond. Culture determines how decisions are made, how conflict is handled, how honor is shown, how worship is expressed, and how leaders are treated.

In apostolic houses, the culture is not defined by convenience or consumerism. It is built by conviction—based on Kingdom values, prophetic vision, and the life of the Spirit.

Apostolic culture includes:

- Honor as the foundation of relationships
- Holiness as the standard, not the exception
- Order that produces peace, not chaos
- Identity rooted in sonship, not performance
- Faith for the impossible, not fear of risk
- Generosity, not self-preservation
- Worship that welcomes glory, not entertainment
- Servanthood that leads, and leadership that serves

And here's the key: culture must be caught, not just taught.

You're Not Just Learning Principles—You're Catching Spirit

In the world, people learn rules and strategies. In the Kingdom, sons and daughters catch spirit. The apostolic house is a place of impartation, not just instruction. That means when you're aligned properly, you don't just hear what your leader says—you catch the way he thinks, the way he responds to pressure, the way he leads, prays, sacrifices, and builds.

This is why proximity without pursuit is dangerous. You can be close in distance but far in spirit. Judas walked with Jesus for three years and never caught His heart. Elisha, on the other hand, refused to leave Elijah's side until he caught both his mantle and his manner.

To catch the culture of your apostolic house, you must:

- Be present and attentive in moments of instruction
- Observe how your leaders operate in different seasons
- Ask questions with humility and hunger
- Serve with consistency and loyalty
- Refuse to adopt outside patterns that contradict the house DNA

Culture isn't transferred through information. It's transferred through spiritual adoption.

Every House Has a Culture—What's Yours?

If you've been planted in an apostolic house, it's your responsibility to know the culture of that house. This is not about personal preference. This is about alignment with the spiritual atmosphere God has chosen to set you in.

Ask yourself:

- How does my leader respond to problems? That becomes my posture.
- How does this house handle worship, prayer, and presence? That becomes my rhythm.
- What language, values, and spiritual priorities are emphasized again and again? That becomes my framework.
- How does this house view discipleship, honor, leadership, giving, and family? That becomes my conviction.

You cannot help build the house if you're not willing to become the house. You can't multiply what you refuse to embody.

Culture Is Caught Through Relationship and Repetition

Culture is not set in a single sermon. It's formed through consistent exposure. Just like a child learns the language of their home without formal education, a spiritual son learns the culture of the house by being around it long enough to absorb it.

That means the team you serve with, the leaders you follow, and the friends you choose all help form and reinforce the culture within you.

Repetition matters. The more you hear something, the more it becomes second nature. When you consistently hear:

- "We honor up, down, and all around"
- "Sons take ownership, not offense"
- "We build with excellence, not excuses"
- "We serve the vision before we start our own"
- "We live from the Spirit, not from the soul"

These phrases don't just shape vocabulary—they embed values. And as you repeat the culture to others, it becomes stronger in you.

Culture Protects the Vision

Culture is what protects vision from erosion. Vision can be written on paper, but culture determines if it becomes reality. Culture ensures that the heart of the house doesn't get lost as it grows.

Without culture, growth becomes cancerous. Gifting replaces character. Systems replace presence. Titles replace servanthood. But when culture is strong, every new team member, disciple, and emerging leader is formed, not just added.

This is why apostolic leaders are fierce about protecting culture. Not because they're insecure or unkind, but because they know that if the culture breaks, the house breaks.

When someone comes into the house with a different culture—dishonor, independence, competition, sloppiness—it's not just "personality"—it's a threat to the foundation.

You cannot build with people who reject the culture. You can love them. Minister to them. Serve them. But you can only build with those who carry the culture.

You Must Become a Carrier of Culture

At some point in your journey from disciple to builder, you stop learning the culture and start carrying it. You don't just model it—you multiply it.

Culture carriers:

- Speak the language of the house
- Correct others with humility when culture is violated
- Protect the leader's voice when gossip arises
- Train others in values, not just tasks
- Smell what doesn't belong and help purify the atmosphere

You don't need a title to be a carrier of culture. You just need faithfulness to what has been entrusted.

The greatest compliment your leader could give you is not "you're talented"—it's "you carry the house."

The Danger of Cultural Drift

Every house will be tested by cultural drift—subtle shifts in values that erode foundations over time.

Cultural drift happens when:

- New people bring in outside mindsets without being retrained
- Offense spreads faster than honor
- People stop serving and start sitting
- Busyness replaces intimacy with God
- Familiarity with the set man breeds dishonor

To fight drift, every leader and disciple must become a guardian of culture. That means constantly asking:

- "Is this still who we are?"
- "Does this reflect our values?"
- "Are we still building the way Heaven showed us?"

The house doesn't stay strong because it has great sermons. It stays strong because its spiritual DNA is guarded.

Culture Creates Family, Not Just Function

Finally, apostolic culture isn't just about excellence or honor—it's about family. Apostles don't just create teams—they build families. And spiritual family is sustained not by function, but by love, loyalty, and shared values.

In apostolic houses, you don't just clock in and clock out.

You are adopted into a rhythm of life that shapes you, challenges you, corrects you, and transforms you. You learn to live like Jesus—laying down your life, preferring others, walking in humility, and staying faithful in every season.

Culture is what makes a house a home. It's what turns servants into sons and visitors into brothers. It's what makes spiritual family possible, not just theoretical.

This Is Who We Are

As you grow in your role within the apostolic house, remember: your primary assignment is not to impress or perform. It is to carry the culture. Become the kind of disciple who embodies the values of the house so deeply that others catch it just by being around you.

You are not just part of a church. You are part of a house with a spiritual blueprint. And that house has a culture worth building, guarding, and multiplying.

So let this be your declaration:

"I don't just serve in this house—I carry the heart of this house.
I don't just know what we do—I know who we are.
And I will build, protect, and multiply that culture—so others can
find home in the presence of God and the family of faith."

Discussion Questions

1. **Catching vs. Creating Culture:** The chapter teaches that *"culture must be caught, not just taught."* What are some practical ways you can catch and embody the culture of your spiritual house? How does this differ from simply learning information or following instructions?

2. **Guarding Against Cultural Drift:** Cultural drift happens subtly—through offense, independence, or familiarity. What are some early signs of drift you've noticed in yourself or in others? How can you actively help guard the atmosphere and values of your house from eroding over time?

3. **Becoming a Carrier of Culture:** The text says, *"The greatest compliment your leader could give you is not 'you're talented'—it's 'you carry the house.'"* What does it mean to truly *carry* the heart and culture of your apostolic family? How might this change the way you serve, lead, and relate to others in the house?

CHAPTER 4

FROM CROWD TO CORE
THE PROCESS OF BEING SET INTO THE HOUSE

I n every apostolic house, there are people at different levels of connection. Some are curious. Some are committed. Some are covenant. The crowd gathers to hear. The core stays to build. The Kingdom doesn't advance through the crowd—it advances through the core. And there is a divine process God uses to transition you from one to the other.

Being "set" into the house is not about joining a team or attending regularly. It is a spiritual act of placement, alignment, and ownership. It's when God moves you from passive participation to purposeful positioning. You stop spectating and start building—not just with your hands, but with your heart, your loyalty, your finances, and your identity.

If you want to be a part of the apostolic team, you must understand this: God is not just looking at your gifts. He's looking at your posture. The road from the crowd to the core is paved with humility, consistency, and submission.

God Doesn't Just Call You to a Church—He Sets You in a House

1 Corinthians 12:18 says, *"But now God has set the members, each one of them, in the body just as He pleased." NKJV*

The word "set" here is not casual—it means to appoint, assign, or establish. You don't set yourself. God sets you. And He doesn't set you based on your preference—He sets you based on His purpose.

The language of Scripture is always about being planted, set, joined, fitly framed together. That speaks of structure, alignment, and design. God doesn't scatter His sons. He places them in a family, under a covering, and in a house where their purpose can be refined and released in order.

Many believers never move beyond the crowd because they resist the process of being set. They want to belong without being accountable. They want to serve without being known. But in apostolic houses, there is no shortcut to the core. You must go through the process of being formed.

The Process: Observation → Participation → Ownership

There is a spiritual process that leads from being a visitor to becoming a builder. You can't bypass it. You must walk it.

1. Observation

This is where most people begin. You're drawn to the house. You're observing the preaching, the leadership, the values. You're feeling the atmosphere, wondering if this is your spiritual family.

This stage is important—but it's not the destination. Observation is not commitment. And God won't unlock authority to someone who only watches from a distance.

Ask yourself: Am I looking for inspiration, or am I ready for transformation?

2. Participation

The next step is engagement. You show up consistently. You start serving. You attend discipleship classes. You come to prayer meetings. You let yourself be known.

This is where the testing begins. The house will expose areas of immaturity, brokenness, and pride. Community doesn't just comfort—it confronts. God starts forming your character in the context of relationships.

But even participation is not the end goal. You can serve without ever catching the spirit of the house. You can participate without taking ownership.

3. Ownership

This is when something shifts. The house becomes your house. The vision becomes your vision. The burden becomes your burden.

You stop waiting to be asked. You start finding what needs to be done.

You stop defending your own ideas. You start defending the culture of the house.

You give, not out of obligation, but out of alignment.

You don't serve for visibility. You serve because you've caught the heart of the set man—and now you carry it.

This is when God sets you. And when you're set, you don't leave casually, complain freely, or live independently.

God Assigns You to Vision, Not Just to People

Many people confuse their attraction to a personality with a divine placement. You may love the way someone preaches. You may resonate with their leadership style. But true spiritual placement is not about personality—it's about vision.

God connects people to apostolic leaders because of the assignment on their life, not just the chemistry of their relationship.
This means:

- You're called to build what that leader is building.
- You're called to catch their heart and serve their mission.
- You're called to submit to the process of being formed in the house God has placed you in.

If you leave the house every time someone offends you or another opportunity looks better, you'll never be set. You'll live in spiritual limbo—gifted, but unrooted; anointed, but unassigned.

Being Set Means Carrying the Burden

When you're set into a house, you carry more than tasks—you carry the weight. You feel it when the house is under attack. You feel it when something is off in the culture. You grieve when people disconnect. You intercede for the leadership. You fight for the vision like it's your own.

This is what separates sons from servants. Sons don't have to be told what to do—they carry the burden of the house. They don't ask, "What's in it for me?" They ask, "How can I serve what God is building here?" They don't serve for applause. They serve because of covenant.

Being Set Requires Sifting and Shaping

Before God sets you, He sifts you. He tests your motives, refines your identity, and breaks off independence.

This is not punishment—it's preparation.

If you're offended by process, you're not ready to be trusted with weight. If you buck under correction, you're not ready for covering. If you expect promotion without proving, you're not ready to be set.

In every apostolic house, the set man is looking for builders, not just helpers. And builders must be formed, not just filled.

Let God break you. Let the house shape you. Let the culture transform you.

The ones who endure the shaping are the ones who get set.

Don't Rush the Process—Honor It

Too many people want to skip the process and get to the

platform. But premature placement is dangerous. It creates pressure without preparation. Responsibility without roots.

Let the Lord set you slowly. Let your roots go deep. Let your soul be healed. Let your motives be purified.

It's not delay—it's design.

The ones who are patient in the process will be planted with permanence.

This Is the Journey from Crowd to Core

You were never meant to stay on the fringes. You were born for covenant. You were born for assignment. You were born to build.

But you must move from:

- Observation to ownership
- Preference to purpose
- Attendance to alignment

Let God set you.
Let your leader form you.
Let the house become your family.
And let the burden of the vision become your joy.

Because once you're set, the house doesn't just carry you—you help carry the house.

Discussion Questions

1. **From Observation to Ownership:** The chapter describes a journey from *observation* → *participation* → *ownership*. Where do you personally find yourself in this process right now? What might God be inviting you to surrender or embrace so that you can move closer to true ownership of the vision?

2. **Purpose Over Preference:** The text says, *"You don't set yourself. God sets you."* How does understanding that truth challenge the way you approach church, leadership, and service? What does it look like to let God—not comfort or convenience—determine your spiritual placement?

3. **Enduring the Sifting and Shaping:** The chapter teaches that before God sets you, He sifts you—testing motives, refining identity, and breaking off independence. What has the sifting process looked like in your life, and how has it prepared you to carry greater spiritual weight with humility and faithfulness?

CHAPTER 5

HOW TO CATCH THE SPIRIT OF YOUR LEADER

Y ou were never called to merely serve your leader's tasks —you were called to carry their spirit. It's one thing to be given assignments. It's another to carry alignment. In apostolic houses, the real impartation doesn't come from doing the work; it comes from catching the spirit of the one God has set to lead.

Elisha didn't just follow Elijah—he caught him. Paul didn't just write letters—he reproduced sons who carried the weight of his vision (Philippians 2:20–22). Jesus didn't just train the Twelve—He shared His Spirit with them. And today, in apostolic houses across the earth, God is still looking for disciples who are not content to be around their leader, but who are hungry to walk in the same spirit.

If you want to move from being useful to being trusted, from being assigned to being appointed, from being in the room to being in the flow, then you must learn how to catch the spirit of your leader.

The Spirit of Your Leader Is Not Their Personality

Let's start with what this does not mean.

Catching your leader's spirit is not about mimicking their style, copying their phrases, or adopting their personality. It's not about sounding like them or dressing like them. That's imitation, not impartation.

To catch your leader's spirit means to carry their heart, think their thoughts, sense what they sense, and bear the weight they carry for the people and the vision.

It's about alignment in:

- Vision — seeing what they see
- Values — loving what they love
- Burden — feeling what they feel
- Posture — responding how they respond
- Spirit — flowing with how they flow

The goal is not to become them. The goal is to move with them, support them, and eventually extend what they carry into new places and new people.

Proximity Is Not the Same as Pursuit

There's a big difference between being close to someone and being connected to their spirit. Judas had proximity to Jesus—but he never carried His heart. Elisha pursued Elijah at every turn, refusing to be left behind, and cried out, "My father, my father!" when Elijah was taken up. He received the double portion—not because he was simply nearby—but because he wanted what was on Elijah's life more than he wanted position, visibility, or convenience.

In apostolic houses, the ones who truly catch the spirit of their leader are those who:

- Stay long enough to endure correction
- Serve faithfully when no one's watching
- Ask questions with hunger, not ambition
- Learn to feel the spiritual weight of the house
- Defend the leader's heart, not just his decisions

Catching the spirit requires pursuit, not just position.

You Don't Just Learn—You Absorb

Catching the spirit of your leader happens through exposure, consistency, and a teachable posture. The more you serve, the more you absorb. You start to hear things before they say them. You anticipate their movements. You begin to pray for the house the way they pray. You see the big picture like they do.

It's not mystical—it's relational and spiritual absorption.

Think about Joshua. He stayed in the tent of meeting even after Moses left (Exodus 33:11). He lingered in the presence Moses lingered in. So when the time came to lead, Joshua didn't just know Moses' methods—he had been marked by Moses' spirit of encounter, order, and obedience.

Many want the results of their leader but are unwilling to walk in the rhythms that shape their leader.

What you hang around long enough, you eventually carry —if your posture is right.

Catching Heart Before Handling Authority

In apostolic houses, authority is never given before heart is proven. Apostolic leaders are not impressed by talent. They are watching for who carries their heart. Can you weep with what makes them weep? Will you fight for what they labor for? Do you protect their blindside or secretly judge it?

Before authority is imparted, heart must be caught.

You can't represent someone you don't understand. And you can't carry weight for someone whose heart you have not pursued.

The set man isn't just looking for volunteers—he's looking for sons who can multiply the vision without mutating the DNA. And that happens through heart connection.

How to Catch the Spirit of Your Leader

So how do you practically do it?

1. Honor Their Voice Above Others

Don't confuse outside influence with inside instruction. Let the voice of your leader be the loudest one shaping how you think, serve, and build. Apostolic sons don't live on a buffet of voices—they carry the recipe of their house.

2. Ask Questions That Reveal Their Heart

Don't just ask, "What do you want me to do?" Ask, "How do you see this? What's the burden here? What are you sensing from God about this area?" Learn how they think, not just what they think.

3. Be Present in Spirit, Not Just in Body

Don't just show up. Be fully present. Engage. Listen. Observe. Ask the Holy Spirit to help you perceive what your leader is carrying—and how you can help hold it up.

4. Stay Long Enough to Be Shaped

You won't catch their spirit in six months. Or even in a year. It takes time. And usually, the process includes offense, correction, pruning, and tension. Those moments aren't disqualifiers —they are tests.

5. Serve What Matters to Them

Look at what your leader values most. Give your strength to it. Whether it's discipleship, prayer, excellence, worship, order, or the health of the house—don't wait to be told. Go above and beyond.

6. Submit Your Gift to Their Government

Your anointing is not the foundation of the house—their vision is. Bring your gift under their government. Be trustworthy in function. Don't compete with what they're building —complement it.

The Cost of Not Catching the Spirit

If you don't catch the spirit of your leader, you'll eventually:

- Misrepresent the house to others
- Create a divided culture through a different tone
- Begin building your own platform within someone else's vision
- Resist correction or accountability
- Reproduce something disconnected from the source

In time, this leads to disconnection, division, or departure —not because of disagreement, but because there was no impartation of spirit. Don't just follow closely—pursue deeply. Don't just do what they say—become what they carry.

Impartation Comes by Honor and Proximity

Paul said of Timothy, "You know his proven character, that as a son with his father he served with me in the gospel" (Philippians 2:22*). This wasn't just partnership—it was spiritual inheritance through proximity and covenant loyalty.

You catch what you honor and serve.

Some want to be poured into, but refuse to carry. Some want the mantle without the maturity. But Elisha received the double portion because he endured the process. He didn't leave when it got inconvenient. He didn't bail when misunderstood. He stuck to Elijah's side—even when others mocked, even when nothing made sense.

And in the end, the mantle found him.

Let This Be Your Pursuit

---

* NKJV

You weren't just called to be in the room. You were called to catch the spirit of your leader. Because when you do, you don't just help build—you help carry the vision.

You don't just serve effectively—you lead consistently. You don't just finish tasks—you extend legacy. So ask the Lord to give you grace to see, to sense, and to serve. Ask for the same spirit your leader walks in. Let it form you, fill you, and flow through you. And as you carry it faithfully, one day others will catch it from you. Because this is how movements multiply—through sons who carry the same spirit.

Discussion Questions

1. **From Tasks to Spirit:** The chapter begins with this truth: *"You were never called to merely serve your leader's tasks—you were called to carry their spirit."* How does this redefine what faithful service looks like in your context? What might need to shift in your mindset or heart posture to move from doing assignments to walking in alignment?

2. **The Difference Between Proximity and Pursuit:** It says, *"Judas had proximity to Jesus—but he never carried His heart."* What does it practically look like to pursue your leader's heart rather than just be near their leadership? How can you cultivate genuine hunger to understand and serve what they carry, rather than simply benefit from their platform?

3. **The Cost and Reward of Catching the Spirit:** The text reminds us that catching the spirit takes time, humility, and endurance through correction and offense. What has this process looked like in your journey of discipleship or leadership? How has God used the challenges of that process to form your heart, refine your motives, and prepare you to carry more weight?

CHAPTER 6

THE POWER OF SUBMISSION AND ALIGNMENT

In the Kingdom, power doesn't begin with position—it begins with posture. If you want to walk in authority, you must learn how to come under authority. If you want to lead, you must first learn how to align. In apostolic houses, the principle of submission and alignment is not an old-fashioned hierarchy—it's a spiritual technology for unlocking access, protection, and purpose.

The truth is simple but sobering: you cannot be trusted to carry the vision if you refuse to submit to the one who carries it. You cannot release Kingdom authority unless you are under Kingdom authority.

God works through order. And alignment is how we posture ourselves in that order—not just with our schedules and responsibilities, but with our hearts.

Submission Is Not Passivity—It's Power Under Control

Submission has been misunderstood and misused. But in the Kingdom, submission doesn't mean you are weak—it means you are willing to yield your strength to serve what is greater than yourself.

Jesus modeled perfect submission. Though He had all power, He said, "I only do what I see the Father doing"*. He wasn't passive—He was power under divine restraint. Submission is not silence or inactivity—it is choosing to bring your will, your gifts, and your passion into agreement with what God has established.

To be submitted is to say:

- "I trust God's order more than my own ambition."
- "I yield my preferences to the process."
- "I don't need to be in charge to be fully engaged."

Submission isn't slavery—it's strategy.

Alignment Unlocks Authority

In Matthew 8, a Roman centurion came to Jesus asking for his servant to be healed. When Jesus offered to come to his house, the centurion replied, "I am a man under authority, and I say to this one 'Go,' and he goes..." (Matthew 8:9 †). Jesus marveled and said, "I have not found such great faith."

Why did this man have such faith? Because he understood the principle of alignment. He wasn't just in authority—he was under authority. And because he was under it, he could flow in it.

---

* Paraphrase John 5:19
† NKJV

In the apostolic house, the same is true. When you are properly aligned:

- You inherit the flow of grace and anointing from the house
- You gain access to resources, counsel, and covering
- You move in spiritual authority that's been tested and trusted

Alignment is not control. It's the divine channel through which delegated authority flows.

If you try to lead apart from alignment, you will eventually burn out, break down, or be bypassed.

Rebellion Blocks the Flow

One of the enemy's oldest strategies is to disrupt divine alignment. From Lucifer's rebellion in heaven to Korah's rebellion against Moses, Satan has always tried to sever what God has joined.

Rebellion is not always loud. Sometimes it whispers. It comes in the form of:

- "I don't need to check in with leadership."
- "I'll do what I feel led to do, regardless of the house."
- "I respect them, but I don't have to submit to everything."

But rebellion is not measured by tone—it's measured by posture.

True submission says: "Even when I don't agree, I yield in

honor because I trust the covering and vision God placed me under."

This doesn't mean leaders are infallible. It means we recognize that God honors alignment, even when we're still processing details.

Those who break rank—spiritually or relationally—end up operating in strange fire. They move independently. They gather people around themselves. They reproduce confusion instead of clarity. And the fruit never lasts.

Alignment Is a Heart Issue, Not Just an Activity

You can be busy serving and still be out of alignment. You can attend every meeting and still have a heart that resists order. You can be visible in function but distant in posture.
Alignment means:

- Your spirit is yielded
- Your heart is teachable
- Your words reflect honor
- Your motives are pure
- Your actions support the vision

It's not about performance—it's about posture.

God doesn't just measure what you do. He measures how you do it. Are you building in unity with the house? Or building something next to it?

Alignment means becoming one with what's been entrusted to the set man, and allowing that alignment to form your rhythms, values, and priorities.

Misalignment Produces Spiritual Tension

Misalignment in the Kingdom is like being out of joint in a physical body. It causes:

- Pain in movement
- Dysfunction in structure
- Weakness in unity
- Exposure to injury

When people are misaligned in the house, everything becomes harder. Communication feels strained. Trust breaks down. Frustration grows. Offense finds a foothold. The house may still function—but not with fullness.

That's why apostolic leaders guard alignment. It's not because they want control—it's because they understand that misalignment compromises spiritual momentum.

God doesn't bless disunity. He blesses oneness.

Submission Is Proven in the Pressing

It's easy to claim submission when everything is going your way. But the true test of submission is when:

- You're corrected
- You're passed over
- You're not given explanation
- You're asked to serve in something you didn't choose

In these moments, your posture is revealed.

True sons don't serve with conditions. They don't demand position. They don't quit when they're challenged.

They understand that submission is part of their transformation. And as they yield, God refines their character, aligns their heart, and prepares them for greater authority.

You can't walk in dominion if you're allergic to submission.

Alignment Brings Access to What You Didn't Build

When you align with the vision and leader God has placed you under, you gain access to spiritual resources you didn't labor for. Just like a branch connected to the vine receives the flow of life (John 15), you step into a spiritual inheritance.

This access includes:

- Covering from demonic attack
- Favor in assignment
- Grace for responsibility
- Doors of opportunity
- Wisdom and discernment
- Blessing on your household

Your alignment becomes a spiritual highway through which God releases provision, authority, and protection.

Don't underestimate the blessing of being rightly aligned.

How to Walk in Submission and Alignment

Here are practical ways to posture your life in submission and alignment:

1. Stay teachable. Don't resist feedback. Let your leaders speak into your life without needing to explain everything to you.
2. Honor privately and publicly. Speak well of your leaders—even when they're not in the room. Let your words reinforce unity.
3. Seek permission, not just blessing. Don't move forward assuming agreement. Submit your ideas and wait for release.
4. Stay planted when pruned. When correction or delay comes, don't uproot. Trust the process.
5. Serve without needing attention. Let your joy be in building the vision—not being recognized for it.
6. Synchronize with the rhythm of the house. Align your priorities with the vision, schedule, and focus of the house.
7. Repent quickly when misaligned. If you sense a heart drift, offense, or independence—bring it into the light and realign.

Alignment Positions You for Promotion

God never promotes outside of order. When He's ready to release you into more, He looks at your alignment, not just your ability.

Faithfulness under another man's vision is what qualifies you for your own (Luke 16:12). But if you try to self-promote before you're set, you step outside the flow.

Apostolic promotion looks like:

- More weight, not more fame
- More responsibility, not just more influence
- More people to serve, not more people serving you

And God gives that kind of promotion to those He can trust. He knows who has learned to submit before they were seen.

This Is the Power of Submission and Alignment

The world teaches independence as maturity.

The Kingdom teaches alignment as maturity.

You don't lose yourself when you submit—you find your place. You don't become invisible—you become entrusted. You don't lose authority—you gain access.

So here's the question:

Are you aligned?

Are you submitted in posture—not just in position?

Are you flowing in unity—or trying to build your own?

Because submission and alignment are not bondage. They are bridges to blessing, authority, and multiplication. And those who walk in them build what lasts.

Discussion Questions

1 . **Power Through Posture:** The chapter opens with, *"In the Kingdom, power doesn't begin with position—it begins with posture."* How does this redefine your view of leadership and influence? What does "power under control" look like in your current season of service or leadership?

2 . **The Test of True Submission:** It says, *"The true test of submission is when you're corrected, passed over, or not given explanation."* Reflect on a time when you faced one of those tests. How did you respond, and what did it reveal about your heart posture toward authority and alignment?

3 . **Alignment as Access:** The text teaches that alignment brings access to what you didn't build—covering, favor, and spiritual inheritance. In what ways have you seen or could you imagine God releasing new grace and opportunity in your life through deeper alignment with your leaders and spiritual house?

CHAPTER 7

STAGES OF MATURITY IN AN APOSTOLIC HOUSE

Maturity is not measured by how long you've been in church, how much Scripture you know, or how loud you pray. In an apostolic house, maturity is measured by trustworthiness, consistency, and your ability to carry weight without compromising the house or yourself.

The journey from being born again to becoming a mature builder in the Kingdom is not instant—it is a process. And this process is not accidental—it is intentional. Apostolic leaders don't just look at your gift; they look at your growth. They're not asking, "Can you preach?" They're asking, "Can you be trusted?"

To understand your journey in the house, you must understand the stages of maturity—because each stage has unique lessons, responsibilities, and temptations. Knowing where you are will help you lean into the process instead of resisting it.

Spiritual Growth is a Pattern of Stages

1 John 2:12–14 gives us a framework for spiritual development:

"I write to you, little children, because your sins are forgiven... I write to you, fathers, because you have known Him... I write to you, young men, because you are strong, and the word of God abides in you, and you have overcome the wicked one." NKJV

From this passage and apostolic observation, we can discern four general stages of spiritual maturity:

1. Infant
2. Child
3. Young Man/Woman
4. Mature Son/Daughter

Each stage represents not only a level of growth but a spiritual posture, and in apostolic houses, each stage must be honored—not skipped or rushed.

1. Infants: Born Again but Not Yet Formed

Every believer starts here. This stage is beautiful, fragile, and critical. Infants in the spirit are like newborns—full of potential, but entirely dependent.
Traits:

- Excited by the newness of faith
- Easily discouraged or confused
- Hungry for love, acceptance, and clarity
- Unfamiliar with spiritual warfare, discipline, or doctrine
- Often governed by emotion rather than conviction

Needs:

- Consistent teaching and nurturing
- A safe place to ask questions
- Affirmation of identity
- Boundaries to protect from confusion

In apostolic houses, infants are not pushed—they're protected. They need grace, not pressure. But they also need intentional discipleship to grow.

Infants are not ready to carry weight. But they must be surrounded by mature examples who model stability and sonship.

2. Children: Learning Identity, Still Centered on Self

Children in the spirit have moved beyond infancy but are still learning how to live from identity, not insecurity. They may know how to pray, serve, or quote Scripture, but they are still developing consistency and emotional health.

Traits:

- Need attention and reassurance
- Struggle with comparison or insecurity
- Begin serving but may still serve to be seen
- Easily offended or confused by correction
- Love the benefits of the house but may not yet carry its burden

Needs:

- Clear boundaries and structure
- Encouragement when corrected

- Teaching on identity, honor, and spiritual discipline
- Exposure to spiritual family, not just leadership

Children must learn how to follow instructions, serve without spotlight, and grow in humility. This is the stage where heart posture begins to take shape, and where submission and consistency are tested.

3. Young Men/Women: Growing in Strength and Overcoming

This stage is marked by strength, responsibility, and testing. You're no longer being held up—you're now being asked to hold up others. But you're still under the supervision of leadership who will test your character, obedience, and trustworthiness.

Traits:

- Strong in the Word and consistent in spiritual disciplines
- Passionate about purpose and making impact
- Learning to overcome spiritual battles and steward authority
- Can handle correction without crumbling
- Begin carrying the weight of culture and leadership

Temptations:

- Pride due to success or visibility
- Frustration at delayed promotion
- Comparison with other leaders or peers
- Independence or desire to "launch out" prematurely

Needs:

- Continued mentorship and accountability
- Opportunities to serve and lead under covering
- Guardrails to prevent burnout or rebellion
- Teaching on legacy, submission, and sonship

Young men and women are vital to apostolic teams. They help build structure, disciple others, and replicate the vision. But they must stay submitted, remain humble, and keep their hearts aligned as they grow.

4. Mature Sons and Daughters: Builders, Fathers, and Culture-Carriers

This is the stage of fruit-bearing, multiplication, and governance. Mature sons and daughters are not just trusted with tasks—they're trusted with people. They carry the spirit of the house, defend its culture, and train others to walk in it.

Traits:

- Steadfast in adversity
- Governed by the Spirit, not by emotion or ambition
- Walk in submission even while leading others
- Speak the language of the house and guard the culture
- Able to father others spiritually and reproduce disciples

Responsibilities:

- Build without ego
- Serve the Set Man's vision without competing
- Protect the house from division, offense, and compromise
- Train up the next generation

- Maintain personal holiness, intimacy, and health

This is not about age—it's about trustworthiness. Mature sons don't need the spotlight. They care more about legacy than applause. And they don't quit when it's hard—they carry the house through storms.

The Apostolic House Honors Process, Not Hype

In the apostolic house, leaders are not chosen by charisma —they are tested through process.

Every stage matters. Rushing someone into leadership before their heart is formed is dangerous—not just for them, but for the whole house. This is why apostles move slowly when releasing authority.

They don't ask:

- "How gifted are you?"

They ask:

- "Can you carry weight without losing alignment?"
- "Do you love correction, or do you merely endure it?"
- "Will you serve the vision when no one's watching?"

Growth isn't about speed. It's about depth. And the deeper your roots go in each stage, the more fruit God can entrust to you.

How to Advance Through the Stages

You don't graduate stages through time—you grow through submission and testing.

Here's how:

1. Stay Planted – Don't uproot when corrected or uncomfortable.
2. Stay Teachable – Don't assume you know more than your leader.
3. Stay Faithful – Be consistent in the small things before asking for big ones.
4. Stay Humble – Let others praise you. Your fruit will speak.
5. Stay in Alignment – Remain under covering, even when you feel ready to "go."

The Kingdom doesn't reward ambition. It promotes faithful sons.

Know Your Stage—Honor the Process

Where are you in the journey?

- Are you still learning to stand?
- Are you wrestling with consistency?
- Are you being tested in responsibility?
- Are you carrying the house for others?

There's no shame in any stage. But there is danger in pretending you're somewhere you're not—or in demanding what you haven't been trusted to carry.

Let the Lord form you. Let your leaders shape you. Let the process mature you into a son who builds what lasts.

Discussion Questions

1. **Measuring Maturity by Trustworthiness:** The chapter begins with the statement that maturity is not measured by knowledge or longevity but by *trustworthiness, consistency, and the ability to carry weight.* How does that definition challenge traditional views of spiritual maturity? In what ways is God currently testing your trustworthiness within your house or assignment?

2. **Recognizing Your Stage of Growth:** The text outlines four stages—Infant, Child, Young Man/Woman, and Mature Son/Daughter. Which stage best describes where you are right now? What are the specific lessons or tests you sense God is emphasizing for you in this season?

3. **Honoring the Process, Not Rushing Promotion:** The chapter says, *"Growth isn't about speed—it's about depth."* How can you cultivate patience and humility in your process of spiritual development? What practical steps can you take to deepen your roots instead of seeking faster recognition or greater visibility?

CHAPTER 8

WHY YOU'RE NOT GIVEN TOO MUCH TOO SOON

There's a deep ache in every maturing disciple for more. More responsibility. More visibility. More authority. More trust. And in a healthy house, that desire is good. It means you're growing. It means you want to carry the weight of Kingdom work.

But in the Kingdom, more is not always now. And in apostolic houses, responsibility is not handed out like candy—it's entrusted through process. God doesn't promote based on gifting. He promotes based on trustworthiness.

If it feels like you've been held back... if you've been wondering why you haven't been given leadership or platform or the "next thing"... this chapter is for you.

You're not being punished.
You're being protected.
You're not being overlooked.
You're being observed—to see if your character can carry what your calling demands.
Because the principle is true: Whatever is gained prema-

turely will eventually crush you if your character isn't ready to carry it.

Gifting Without Grounding Is Dangerous

One of the most sobering patterns in Scripture and history is this: people who are gifted but not grounded end up harming both themselves and the people they were called to serve.

Think of Saul. He was anointed before he was mature. And because of his insecurity, pride, and disobedience, the kingdom was ripped away from him.

Contrast that with David. Anointed young—but entrusted later. He served. He waited. He submitted. He carried another man's armor before he wore his own crown. And even when Saul tried to kill him, David refused to take the throne prematurely.

In apostolic houses, wise leaders follow this pattern. They don't release people based on potential. They release people based on proven character.

Waiting Is a Test, Not a Denial

You may be gifted. You may be anointed. You may have dreams, prophecies, and supernatural encounters that affirm your calling. And all of those may be true. But none of those are proof that you're ready. Time is the great revealer. Delay exposes motives. Tests refine character.

And seasons of hiddenness aren't just frustrating—they're formative.

- God is stretching your humility.
- He's building your endurance.
- He's checking your posture under pressure.
- He's letting your roots grow deep before your fruit grows wide.

If you're truly called, your gift will still be there when the time is right.

The waiting doesn't disqualify you—it develops you.

Why Apostolic Leaders Restrict Responsibility

In apostolic houses, you don't get promoted by volunteering more or being the loudest in the room. You get promoted through:

- Submission
- Trustworthiness
- Consistency
- Alignment

Apostolic leaders carry the weight of the house. That means they're not just thinking about whether you're ready—they're thinking about what your elevation would do to:

- The culture
- The team dynamic
- The spiritual health of the house
- The vision God gave them

If you're held back, it's not because they don't see your potential—it's because they're protecting what God entrusted to them, and possibly protecting you from yourself.

Trust the covering. Trust the process. And remember: nothing healthy is built in haste.

God Uses Delay to Reveal What You Can't See

If God gave you everything you wanted right now—the mic, the influence, the leadership mantle—what would it reveal in you?

Would it expose pride?
Would it feed insecurity?
Would it become your identity?
Would it change your posture toward those you once served with?

That's why God delays. Because He wants you stronger than your stage.

He wants your soul anchored, not inflated.
He wants your gift to serve others, not yourself.
You're not waiting for God to open a door.
God is waiting for your inner life to catch up with your outer assignment.

Restriction Is Love in Disguise

When a father says "not yet" to a child asking for the car keys, that's not rejection—it's love.
When your apostolic leader says:

- "Serve here for a while longer"
- "Let's wait before releasing you into that"
- "This isn't the season for that opportunity"

...what they're really saying is:

"I love you too much to let you crash under the weight of something you're not ready to carry."

In immature environments, people are promoted too quickly and burned too fast. In apostolic houses, things may move slower, but what's built lasts.

Because love says: I'd rather grow you than impress others with you.

Assignment Always Comes After Alignment

Don't chase opportunities. Chase alignment.

Don't pursue your next role. Pursue faithfulness in your current one.

Because in the Kingdom:

- You don't graduate by asking for more—you graduate by being faithful with less.
- You don't get handed influence because you're frustrated—you get it because you've been formed by process.
- You don't lead because you desire leadership—you lead because your life proves trustworthy.

If your heart is aligned, your assignment will find you.

The Dangers of Premature Promotion

When people are promoted too soon, a few things usually happen:

1. They burn out — The weight they carry drains them because they don't yet have the spiritual structure to sustain it.
2. They fall morally or emotionally — The visibility feeds pride or exposes unresolved wounds.
3. They damage others — Their decisions aren't guided by wisdom, and those under them suffer the consequences.
4. They divide the house — They draw others to themselves, creating cultures around gifting instead of around the Set Man's vision.

This is why your leaders—and God Himself—are protecting you with restriction. Because what looks like delay is actually grace.

God Will Not Release What Your Character Cannot Carry

Anointing may open doors. But only character keeps them open. Many people can preach well. Few can lead well under pressure. Many people are gifted in the Spirit. Few can remain grounded when attacked, overlooked, or misunderstood.

In apostolic houses, your character is not just a suggestion —it's a prerequisite.

You're not waiting for permission—you're being forged for promotion.

This Is Why You're Not Given Too Much Too Soon

Not because you're not called.
Not because you're not gifted.
Not because you're being punished.
But because the house loves you enough to form you first.
So don't despise the season of hiddenness.
Don't chase platforms.
Don't assume "next" means "now."

Instead:

- Lean into the slow work of the Spirit.
- Let your roots go deep.
- Serve with joy in obscurity.
- Let honor and humility be your reward.
- Let God build you before He builds through you.

Because when your time comes—when your leader sees that your heart, posture, and character have been tested—you won't have to promote yourself.

You'll be trusted.
You'll be released.
And you'll be ready.

Discussion Questions

1. **Protected, Not Punished:** The chapter reminds us that *"You're not being punished—you're being protected."* How does that perspective change the way you interpret seasons of delay, hiddenness, or restriction? Can you recall a time when what felt like denial was actually God's protection or preparation?

2. **Gifting vs. Grounding:** It says, *"Whatever is gained prematurely will eventually crush you if your character isn't ready to carry it."* What areas of your life or ministry might need deeper grounding before greater responsibility? How can you partner with God in developing the maturity and character that sustain promotion?

3. **Faithfulness Before Promotion:** The chapter concludes, *"Let God build you before He builds through you."* What does that practically look like in your current season? How can you stay faithful, joyful, and teachable while waiting for God's timing and your leader's release?

CHAPTER 9
FROM HELPER TO STEWARD — GROWING IN RESPONSIBILITY

E very house begins with helpers. But not every helper becomes a steward. One is given a task. The other carries a burden. One follows instruction. The other anticipates need. In the apostolic house, there comes a moment when God calls every disciple to transition—not just in function, but in identity. From servant to steward. From doing to owning. From merely helping to carrying the house as your own.

This chapter is about that shift. A sacred pivot point in your journey of maturity. A call to grow not just in skills or time spent, but in responsibility—with the heart of a son or daughter who knows they're building legacy.

From Needing Instruction to Becoming an Example

In the early days, helpers need instruction. They ask what to do, when to show up, and how to do it. That's healthy. In fact, asking questions, receiving training, and being coached is how humility is formed and fruitfulness begins.

But if five years later you're still waiting for someone to tell you where the mop is, something's off.

Stewards grow into initiative. They stop waiting to be asked and start anticipating what's needed. They don't just do what's told—they become an example for others to follow.
As Paul said to Timothy:

> *"Set an example for the believers in speech, in conduct, in love, in faith and in purity"* (1 Timothy 4:12, NIV)

Stewardship begins when others start to look to you—not just for instructions—but for inspiration. It's when your life becomes a training manual. When your serving trains others without words. When your consistency becomes a stabilizing force in the culture.

Helpers follow. Stewards lead.

Serving Vision Before Starting Your Own

In today's culture, we glorify the self-made leader—the entrepreneur, the trailblazer, the "start something new" anointing. But in the Kingdom, faithfulness precedes fruitfulness. And before God gives you your own vision to lead, He asks: Can you serve someone else's?

This is the Joseph principle. Before Joseph led Egypt, he stewarded Potiphar's house and managed the prison. He proved he could multiply someone else's vision without needing credit. And it was that faithfulness that qualified him for elevation.
Jesus affirmed this Kingdom principle:

"And if you have not been faithful in what is another man's, who will give you what is your own?" (Luke 16:12, NKJV)

Stewards understand this. They don't serve with secret resentment, wondering when their "real" ministry will start. They serve with joy, knowing that God promotes those who build with loyalty, excellence, and honor.

Your future is hidden in your current stewardship.

Owning the Burden of the House

Helpers clock in. Stewards carry the weight.

There's a shift that happens in every true son or daughter: one day, they don't just serve the vision—they ache for it. When the house is under attack, they intercede. When people are struggling, they follow up. When something's not working, they fix it without needing a title or a pat on the back.

It's not because they're trying to impress. It's because they've taken ownership.

This is how Paul described Timothy:

"I have no one else like him, who will show genuine concern for your welfare. For everyone looks out for their own interests, not those of Jesus Christ" (Philippians 2:20–21, NIV)

Timothy carried Paul's heart. He was a steward of the apostolic burden. He didn't just execute tasks—he carried the heartbeat of the house.

When you begin to weep over what your leader weeps

over... when you defend what he or she defends... when you start building not because you were told to, but because it's your house too—you're not a helper anymore.

You're a steward.

Faithfulness Unlocks Trust

At the end of the day, stewardship is about trust. Helpers are appreciated. But stewards are trusted. That's why Jesus said:

"Well done, good and faithful servant; you were faithful over a few things, I will make you ruler over many things" (Matthew 25:21, NKJV)

This principle is eternal. Faithfulness leads to increase. Not just in opportunity, but in responsibility. Not just more to do, but more to carry. More people. More spiritual weight. More authority.

You don't earn trust by demanding it. You receive it through longevity, integrity, and consistency—especially when no one's watching.

Stewardship is the path to multiplication.

You Can Be a Steward Without a Title

You don't need a mic to have authority. You don't need a platform to carry weight. In the apostolic house, stewards are recognized not just by their gifting—but by their spirit.

Some of the most powerful stewards in a house are never on stage. They set the spiritual temperature, enforce the values, mentor the next generation, and build the walls with hidden faithfulness.

In fact, many of the titles and promotions in the Kingdom come after you've already been functioning in that role for a long time.

Apostles don't appoint based on hype. They appoint based on proven track record.

So if you feel overlooked, ask yourself:

- Have I been stewarding the current assignment with joy?
- Have I allowed offense, comparison, or impatience to creep in?
- Have I been serving to be seen—or because I love the house?

God sees. God rewards. And God promotes.

When You Become the Example Others Watch

There's a holy weight that rests on those who mature in stewardship: you're no longer just a disciple—you're a living blueprint. Others are now patterning their walk after you.

That's what Paul meant when he wrote:

"Imitate me, just as I also imitate Christ" (I Corinthians II:I, NKJV)

This is not arrogance. It's apostolic responsibility.

Stewards are those who now shape culture. Their yes sets

the tone. Their lifestyle becomes contagious. Their presence brings stability. They don't just do ministry—they become the model of it.

From Helping in the Moment to Building for the Future

The difference between a helper and a steward often comes down to timeline.

Helpers focus on the immediate need. Stewards think long-term. They're not just trying to survive Sunday—they're asking: "How do we build for the next five years?"

They see cracks in the wall and offer solutions. They notice gaps in the team and mentor others. They spot the next generation rising and begin training them before they're ever asked.

Stewards think like architects, not just volunteers. This kind of thinking creates legacy. And legacy is the true fruit of an apostolic house.

Questions for Reflection

1. Am I still waiting to be told what to do, or have I stepped into ownership?
2. Do I carry the vision as my own, or do I see it as someone else's?
3. Have I asked God to increase my spiritual responsibility—or just my visibility?
4. Have I started building others like I've been built?

Activation: From Helper to Steward

Take these next steps intentionally:

- Ask your apostolic leader or pastor: "What is something I can carry so you don't have to?"
- Identify one area of the house where you can grow from 'doing' to 'owning.'
- Begin training someone in what you've already learned. If you're a steward, you should be raising other stewards.

The goal isn't just to do more. It's to carry more with the right heart. Because in the end, the house isn't built by the gifted—it's built by the faithful. And if you'll steward what belongs to another, God will entrust you with what has your name on it.

Discussion Questions

1 . **From Doing to Owning:** The chapter says, *"One is given a task. The other carries a burden."* Where in your current service are you still functioning like a helper, and where have you begun to carry the burden of a steward? What would it look like for you to shift from doing what's asked to anticipating and owning the needs of the house?

2 . **Faithfulness Before Fruitfulness:** The text reminds us, *"Before God gives you your own vision to lead, He asks: Can you serve someone else's?"* How are you currently stewarding what belongs to another? In what ways might God be shaping your future leadership through your faithfulness in this season?

3 . **Becoming the Example:** The chapter states, *"Stewards are those who now shape culture. Their yes sets the tone."* How does that truth challenge the way you show up in your house, team, or ministry? What areas of your life or attitude need refining so your example consistently reflects the heart and culture of the house?

CHAPTER 10

THE APOSTOLIC TEAM
BUILDERS, NOT JUST BELIEVERS

Builders Are Different Than Believers. In the Church today, many are content to believe—but few are committed to build. There's a massive difference between those who attend a house and those who help construct it. Believers are recipients of grace; builders are stewards of it. Apostolic teams don't just celebrate salvation—they co-labor with Christ to expand His Kingdom on Earth.

Jesus never told His disciples to merely "make believers." He commissioned them to make disciples. And discipleship is not passive. It requires movement, mission, and multiplication. Apostolic teams embody this spirit. They are marked not just by devotion, but by contribution—by taking ownership of the Father's business and building together as one.

Apostolic Houses Require Apostolic Teams

Just as Jesus built with a team of twelve, and Paul traveled with apostolic company, every apostolic house must be anchored by a team—men and women who have caught the vision, aligned with the leader, and carry delegated authority to build, disciple, and govern.

An apostolic team is not a group of talented individuals gathered around a personality. It is a spiritual family aligned around a divine blueprint. These are sons and daughters who walk in honor, steward culture, and multiply the Father's heart in new places, ministries, and people. They don't just represent leadership; they carry the government of Heaven into every assignment.

The Fivefold Synergy — One Mission, Many Functions

Apostolic teams are made strong through diversity. Ephesians 4:11–13 tells us that Christ gave the fivefold ministry—apostles, prophets, evangelists, pastors, and teachers—for the equipping of the saints and the building up of the Body of Christ.

Each grace has its own role:

- Apostles govern and pioneer. They lay foundations and steward blueprints.
- Prophets guide and clarify. They bring the voice of Heaven into decisions and direction.
- Evangelists gather and expand. They reach the lost and ignite passion for the harvest.
- Pastors guard and nurture. They shepherd the people and steward relational health.
- Teachers ground and explain. They equip the saints in the Word and doctrine.

Apostolic teams function best when these roles are honored, aligned, and submitted to the apostolic vision. There is no competition in a Kingdom house. Each grace adds strength and clarity to the others. Together, they don't just maintain—they multiply.

Moving from Ministry to Government

The Church is not just a spiritual hospital—it is also Heaven's embassy on Earth. Apostolic teams don't just heal wounds; they establish government. They discern the territory, define spiritual jurisdiction, and carry out Kingdom strategy under apostolic oversight.

A team must move beyond ministry events and programs into apostolic governance. This means understanding when to set elders, raise deacons, appoint house pastors, and release spiritual sons into new territories. These are not merely administrative functions—they are spiritual mandates that require discernment, alignment, and maturity.

In an apostolic house, teams are not built to maintain internal order only; they are raised to expand the rule of Christ in homes, cities, and nations.

Becoming a Builder: The Heart of the Team

So what marks a true builder in an apostolic house?

1. Builders Take Ownership
2. They don't just do what's assigned—they care deeply about the success of the house. They ask, "What more can I do? What's not being seen? How can I help carry the burden of the Set Man?" Ownership is the fruit of sonship.
3. Builders Carry Culture

4. They don't bring in other blueprints. They embody the language, values, and convictions of the house. Their speech, service, and spirit are aligned with what the apostle carries.

5. Builders Are Humble and Hungry

6. They don't demand position. They serve faithfully and let promotion come from God. They hunger to grow, to be equipped, and to be trusted with greater weight.

7. Builders Multiply Others

8. They aren't content to serve alone. They raise up others, disciple new leaders, and impart what they've caught. Builders aren't just workers—they're reproducers.

9. Builders Protect What's Sacred

10. They watch for dishonor, gossip, or seeds of division and confront them in love. Builders know that what you build through years of faithfulness can be broken in moments of compromise or offense.

Team Unity: One Heart, One Mind

In Acts 4:32, the early believers were described as being "of one heart and one soul." This wasn't surface-level unity—it was spiritual oneness born from covenant and Kingdom vision. That kind of unity is essential for apostolic teams.

Unity doesn't mean uniformity. It means oneness of purpose, spirit, and direction. Apostolic teams know how to submit preferences for the sake of the greater call. They don't sabotage vision with selfish ambition. They honor one another's gifts while yielding to apostolic authority and collective discernment.

This unity releases power. When the team is one, God commands His blessing (Psalm 133). The house becomes a dwelling place for God's glory and a launching pad for transformation.

A Team That Multiplies the Kingdom

An apostolic team is never called to just sustain the status quo. They are called to expand. The goal is not to get comfortable but to multiply the culture, plant new works, raise new leaders, and equip the saints for every good work.

Multiplication happens through the sons of the house—those who've been faithful with little and are now entrusted with much. These sons don't start rogue movements—they're sent by the apostle. They don't disconnect from their root system—they reproduce it in new soil.

This is how movements are born. Not from ambition, but from alignment. Not from hype, but from honor. Apostolic teams that stay together, grow together, and go together will multiply far beyond what any single person could build alone.

Your Role in the Team

Maybe you're reading this and you're part of a house that is apostolic in nature. Maybe your pastor is an apostle who's carrying vision far bigger than what one man can build alone. Maybe you've sensed the call to rise—not just as a believer, but as a builder.

Let this chapter stir something deep in you. Your church is not just a gathering place—it's an apostolic center. Your leader is not just a preacher—they're a builder of movements. Your role is not just to attend—it's to build.

Builders aren't perfect. They're available. They're loyal. They're growing. And they're willing to pour their lives into something bigger than themselves.

You have a place on the team. The question is: will you take your place and help build what Heaven has blueprint?

Discussion Questions

1 . **From Believer to Builder:** The chapter says, *"Believers are recipients of grace; builders are stewards of it."* In what ways is God calling you to shift from simply receiving to actively building? How can you begin taking ownership of the Father's business in your local house or team?

2 . **Honoring Diversity, Guarding Unity:** The fivefold ministry functions (apostle, prophet, evangelist, pastor, teacher) are designed to complement one another, not compete. Which of these graces do you most identify with, and how can you better align and serve the others to strengthen the whole team's unity and effectiveness?

3 . **Building Through Alignment, Not Ambition:** The text says, *"Movements are born not from ambition, but from alignment."* What does that statement mean to you personally? How can you guard your heart from striving or self-promotion and instead cultivate alignment, humility, and honor within your team?

CHAPTER 11
COMMUNICATION, CORRECTION, AND COVENANT
COMMUNICATION THAT BUILDS, NOT BREAKS

I n any apostolic house, clear and Kingdom-aligned communication is not optional—it's essential. Communication is more than words exchanged; it's the way hearts are aligned, expectations are clarified, and vision is transmitted. In teams led by apostles, where spiritual authority and relational connection go hand in hand, miscommunication can quickly fracture what God is building.

Jesus modeled open, honest, and honoring communication with His disciples. He spoke plainly to them, asked questions to expose motives, and used words to build them up—even when He was correcting them. In the same way, teams built on apostolic foundations must learn to speak the truth in love (Ephesians 4:15), with both clarity and compassion.

Healthy communication means we avoid the two ditches: silence that allows bitterness to grow and explosive speech that wounds others. Apostolic teams thrive when communication is intentional, not reactionary; proactive, not passive-aggressive. When problems arise, we don't gossip about them—we go to the person, not around them.

Correction as a Gift, Not a Curse

Correction is one of the greatest tests of sonship. How someone receives correction reveals the posture of their heart: whether they are acting like a servant, an orphan, or a son. Servants obey out of fear. Orphans defend or withdraw. But sons lean in, trusting that correction is a sign of love, not rejection.

Hebrews 12:6 reminds us: "For whom the Lord loves He chastens."* The same principle applies in apostolic leadership. Fathers in the faith correct because they care. Apostolic correction is not punitive—it's restorative. It doesn't crush identity; it refines character and restores alignment.

However, not all correction is created equal. It must be done in the right spirit, the right timing, and with the right language. Correction without relationship feels like rejection. That's why apostles and leaders in the house must build enough relational equity that when correction comes, it lands as care, not control.

Sons Embrace Correction, Orphans Resist It

One of the clearest differences between sons and orphans is how they respond to correction. Sons have a posture of humility and hunger. They ask, "What can I learn from this? How can I grow?" Orphans, by contrast, see correction as an attack. They get defensive, offended, or distant.

In a healthy apostolic house, correction is expected, welcomed, and even pursued. Sons aren't waiting for someone to tell them they're off—they're asking, "How can I serve better?

---

* NKJV

Where am I missing it?" This humility accelerates maturity and trust.

True sons even invite correction because they know it's part of their development. Like Timothy, who received strong words from Paul, they understand that correction is not rejection—it's preparation for greater responsibility.

Creating a Culture of Feedback

In the apostolic team, feedback should not be feared—it should be normalized. This starts with leaders creating space for honest conversations, not just top-down direction. It also requires teaching team members how to give feedback in an honoring and constructive way.

When leaders can be corrected by those under them (appropriately), and when sons can be sharpened by brothers and sisters on the team, the house becomes stronger. Everyone is committed not just to being right, but to building right.

Feedback should follow this pattern:

1. Honor first – Acknowledge what's good.
2. Be specific – Don't generalize problems; define them.
3. Speak to purpose – Connect correction to the bigger vision.
4. End in hope – Remind them of who they are and who they're becoming.

Covenant Relationships That Endure Storms

Apostolic houses don't function like businesses or casual ministry teams—they're built on covenant. Covenant is not convenience; it's commitment. It's the kind of bond where you say, "I'm not leaving because it gets hard. I'm staying because God has joined us."

Jesus didn't say, "I'll be with you as long as you don't mess up." He said, "I will never leave you nor forsake you." This covenant mindset must shape the way apostolic teams relate. We don't abandon each other when misunderstandings happen. We press in, pursue reconciliation, and fight for unity.

Covenant means we show up. We speak up. We forgive quickly. We don't harbor hidden offenses. We recognize that Satan's number one strategy to stop a move of God is to divide the team through unresolved pain and relational fractures.

Confronting in a Spirit of Honor

When confrontation is necessary—and it will be—it must be done with the spirit of honor. That means we confront for the sake of the person and the purpose, not for revenge or to vent emotion. We are not trying to win an argument; we're fighting for the relationship.

Galatians 6:1 gives us the tone: "If anyone is caught in a trespass, you who are spiritual should restore him in a spirit of gentleness."* Apostolic leadership requires spiritual maturity to correct without crushing, and boldness to not avoid necessary conversations.

Honor doesn't mean we avoid hard truths. It means we speak those truths in a way that calls someone up, not tears them down.

---

* NASB

When Sons Correct Their Leaders

Even in covenant relationships, sons sometimes need to bring concerns to their spiritual fathers or team leaders. The key is how they do it. Rebellion sounds like accusation; honor sounds like a question. Rebellion exposes in public; honor approaches in private.

Mature sons carry a posture that says, "I trust your heart, and I just want to share what I'm seeing." If there's blind spots in a leader's leadership, a true son will bring it with humility, prayer, and a heart to build, not tear down.

Leaders who are secure in their identity will welcome this kind of feedback. Apostolic leaders are not infallible—they are human, and covenant protects them too. The team becomes a safeguard when everyone walks in truth and love.

The Danger of Silent Offense

One of the greatest threats to apostolic teams is unspoken offense. When someone gets hurt and doesn't talk about it, bitterness takes root. Offense opens the door to disconnection, and disconnection opens the door to division.

The enemy doesn't need to destroy a team to neutralize it—he just needs to isolate its members emotionally. When people stop communicating, stop trusting, or start making assumptions, they begin withdrawing spiritually.

That's why in apostolic culture, offense is not allowed to fester. We go quickly to one another. We say, "This hurt me," or "Can I clarify what you meant?" We protect our covenant through communication.

Covenants Are for the Long Haul

Kingdom relationships are not just assignments—they're alignments. Apostolic houses are not launching pads for people to jump ship when they feel done. They are places of deep formation, lifelong relationships, and generational legacy.

Yes, there are times when God transitions people. But healthy transitions happen in honor and release, not in anger and rebellion. Covenant relationships seek clarity and closure. They leave with blessing, not burned bridges.

When someone leaves without a conversation, without a blessing, or with accusation in their heart, they're not just walking out the door—they're breaking covenant. And broken covenants carry consequences in the spirit.

Building a Culture That Lasts

If you want to build a team that lasts, you must build on covenant, not convenience. That means you'll need to have hard conversations, pursue people who withdraw, and refuse to let misunderstanding grow into bitterness.

But the reward is this: a family that builds for decades, not months. A team that governs cities, not just Sunday services. A people who know how to confront and stay connected, how to correct and stay humble, how to build without breaking each other.

This is the apostolic way. Communication. Correction. Covenant.

Discussion Questions

1. **The Power of Honest Communication:** The chapter begins by saying that communication is how *"hearts are aligned, expectations are clarified, and vision is transmitted."* Where have you seen healthy or unhealthy communication shape a team or ministry? What habits could you personally strengthen to build clearer, more Kingdom-aligned communication in your relationships and team?

2. **Correction Reveals Sonship:** It says, *"How someone receives correction reveals whether they are acting like a servant, an orphan, or a son."* How do you usually respond when corrected or challenged? What would it look like for you to fully embrace correction as a gift that brings growth rather than as criticism that brings shame?

3. **Covenant That Endures Conflict:** The text teaches that covenant means *"I'm not leaving because it gets hard. I'm staying because God has joined us."* How can you personally model covenant relationships when conflict or offense arises? What practical steps can you take to protect unity and confront issues in a spirit of honor and humility?

CHAPTER 12

GUARDING THE HOUSE — LOYALTY, HONOR, AND WARFARE
THE WEIGHT OF WHAT WE CARRY

E very apostolic house is entrusted with something sacred —a word, a vision, a culture, a people. It is not just a ministry; it is a divine assignment. And like anything precious in the Kingdom, it attracts warfare. What God builds, the enemy always tries to break. What God joins, Satan tries to divide. What God births, the adversary seeks to abort. This is why guarding the house is not optional for those who belong to it. It's a responsibility every son and daughter must embrace.

In Scripture, Nehemiah's wall wasn't just about protection —it was about identity. The wall marked who the people were and what belonged to them. Without the wall, the people were vulnerable to invasion and confusion. In the same way, the spiritual "walls" of a house—the boundaries of culture, honor, order, and spiritual authority—must be vigilantly guarded, not just by the set man, but by every builder on the team.

Protecting the Vision and the Voice of the House

Every house has a voice—a sound that reflects the Spirit, assignment, and identity of that house. When that voice is clear, the people are united. When it's confused or contradicted, the people scatter. Guarding the house begins with guarding the voice.

The voice of the house is often carried first by the apostolic leader—the set man who has received the blueprint from God. But as the house matures, that voice must also be carried by the team, by spiritual sons, by leaders who echo—not parrot—the sound of Heaven for that family. This includes guarding how the vision is spoken about, what is taught, what is corrected, and what is passed on.

To protect the voice, we must silence other competing voices—especially gossip, slander, comparison, and divisive opinions. Paul warned the church in Corinth that "there are many voices in the world, and none of them is without significance" (1 Cor. 14:10). But not every voice belongs in the house. Just because someone has a microphone on Instagram doesn't mean they have a mandate in your house.

When someone consistently critiques the voice of the house, they are not just offering a different opinion—they may be challenging divine order. And when that goes unaddressed, it begins to subtly erode confidence in leadership and undermine the grace flowing through proper alignment. We must be bold in love to protect the stream God has established.

Loyalty Is Not Silence—It's Spirit-to-Spirit Honor

In today's culture, loyalty is often misunderstood. It's seen as blind agreement or passive compliance. But biblical loyalty is neither of those things. Loyalty is not silence—it is spirit-to-spirit honor. It's the ability to stand with your leader, your house, and your team, not just in the spotlight but in the shadows. It's choosing to believe the best, protect the vulnerable, and stay planted when it would be easier to walk away.

Jonathan's loyalty to David was not expressed through flattery but through covenant. When Saul tried to destroy David, Jonathan protected him—not out of rebellion, but out of divine recognition. He discerned who carried the oil. True loyalty flows from revelation.

Spirit-to-spirit honor means you see your leaders, your house, your brothers and sisters by the Spirit—not through carnal filters. You choose to cover, not expose. To build, not break. To believe, not betray. Honor is not just about words; it's about posture. When correction comes, honor leans in. When misunderstanding arises, honor seeks clarity—not a crowd.

One of the great tests of loyalty is how we speak about the house when we're outside of it. Do we defend it in conversations? Do we shut down dishonor in private? Do we echo the culture and convictions of our spiritual family when no one is watching?

The Enemy's Strategy: Offense and Disconnection

Satan doesn't need to destroy an apostolic house if he can divide it. He doesn't need to overthrow leadership if he can sow subtle discontentment. His favorite tools in mature churches are not always sin—they are offense, comparison, and disconnection.

Jesus warned, "It is impossible that no offenses should come" (*Luke 17:1). Offense is inevitable—but how you handle

---

* NKJV

it determines your spiritual maturity. Sons bring offense into the light. Servants harbor it in silence. Offense that's not addressed turns into suspicion. Suspicion turns into accusation. Accusation births disconnection.

In apostolic houses, disconnection often begins emotionally long before it becomes physical. A leader stops leaning in. A son stops initiating. A once-vocal team member becomes quiet and disengaged. The root isn't always rebellion—it may be unhealed offense.

The enemy thrives in isolation. Just like a predator seeks to pull the weak one from the herd, Satan looks for those who have withdrawn in their spirit. That's where he whispers lies: "They don't see you," "You don't belong here," "You're more anointed than them," "You're just being used." These are not just thoughts —they are seeds from hell intended to destroy covenant.

The remedy is humility and conversation. When offense arises, run to the light. When suspicion creeps in, ask questions —not other people, but the one you're suspicious of. Apostolic culture doesn't avoid hard conversations—it invites them. When we value relationship over being right, the house is strengthened, not weakened.

Watchmen on the Wall

Guarding the house is not just the role of the set man—it's the responsibility of every member who calls it home. In Ezekiel 33, God speaks to the watchman on the wall. If he sees danger and does not sound the alarm, he is held accountable for the people's blood. But if he warns them, and they don't listen, he is free of guilt.

Every mature believer is a watchman. You don't just attend church—you watch over it. When you sense danger, disorder, disunity, or deception, you don't gossip about it—you sound the alarm. Not in panic, but in prayer. Not in slander, but in submission to order.

Some guard the house through intercession. Others through correction. Others by simply keeping their heart pure and their spirit sweet. But all of us must be on the wall. The Kingdom is too precious, the vision too sacred, and the souls too valuable to be careless.

Guarding in the Spirit and in the Natural

While guarding begins in the spirit, it manifests in practical ways. A culture of protection includes:

- Guarding the front door: Who do we allow to lead, to speak, to influence?
- Guarding the back door: Do we notice when someone is slipping away? Do we chase the one?
- Guarding the team: Do we shut down gossip and offense quickly?
- Guarding the values: Are we training new people in the DNA, or assuming they'll just "catch it"?
- Guarding the altar: Are we praying, fasting, interceding over the atmosphere of our gatherings?

Apostolic houses thrive not just because of powerful Sundays—but because of protective sons. When leaders don't have to constantly guard their backs, they can face the future with boldness. When team members carry the weight of the house together, momentum increases. And when correction and covering flow freely, the house becomes a fortress, not just a gathering.

The Reward of a Guarded House

When a house is guarded in loyalty and honor, glory can dwell there. Psalm 133 says that where there is unity, "the Lord commands the blessing—life forevermore.*" Unity doesn't mean uniformity—it means alignment. It means the people are moving with one heart, one sound, one purpose. That's the kind of house God entrusts with His presence, His people, and His power.

In guarded houses, the prophetic flows without mixture. Disciples are raised without compromise. Fivefold teams grow without division. Sons are sent without fear of rebellion. Because everyone knows—the vision is safe here. The culture is clear here. The leadership is protected here. And Heaven is pleased here.

Closing Charge: Stand Guard

If you've been planted in an apostolic house, you are not just a consumer of vision—you are a guardian of it. You are not just a receiver of culture—you are a reproducer and a protector. Guard it with your speech. Guard it with your relationships. Guard it with your prayers. Guard it with your obedience. Guard it by staying connected, corrected, and aligned.

The enemy may not fear big churches—but he fears united houses. Houses where sons don't scatter. Houses where correc-

---

* NKJV

isn't punishment, but protection. Houses where vision doesn't get diluted by offense or divided by ambition.

Be a son who guards. Be a builder who protects. Be a watchman who sees. And together, we will see the house of the Lord stand strong in every season.

Discussion Questions

1. **Protecting What's Sacred:** The chapter says, *"What God builds, the enemy always tries to break."* What are some practical and spiritual ways you can personally help guard the vision, the voice, and the culture of your house? How can you become more alert to subtle forms of attack like gossip, comparison, or offense?

2. **Loyalty as Spirit-to-Spirit Honor:** It teaches that *"Loyalty is not silence—it's spirit-to-spirit honor."* How does that redefine your understanding of loyalty and submission? In what ways can you demonstrate true honor to your leaders and your team, especially when facing misunderstandings or correction?

3. **Becoming a Watchman:** The text declares that *"Every mature believer is a watchman."* What does being a spiritual watchman look like in your role—whether in prayer, intercession, accountability, or protecting relationships? How can you strengthen your vigilance without slipping into suspicion or control?

CHAPTER 13
SONS, NOT SLAVES — SERVING FROM INHERITANCE, NOT OBLIGATION

There is a vast difference between someone who is loyal out of duty and someone who is faithful out of love. In the Kingdom of God, motivation is not a footnote—it's the foundation. The apostolic house is not built by obligation but by inheritance. It's not built by people who feel pressured to perform but by sons and daughters who carry the heart of the house as their own.

Sons Take Ownership, But Don't Take Over

Apostolic houses thrive when people serve with the spirit of sonship—not entitlement, not insecurity, and certainly not ambition. Sons don't fight to be noticed. They don't jostle for position. They know that their place is secured by relationship, not by manipulation. A slave must compete for his survival. A son rests in his inheritance.

Sons take ownership, not to control, but to carry. They care about the church bathrooms because they care about the church body. They notice what's missing because they know they're called to fill it. They step up—not because someone asked them, but because something in them knows. They are home, and when something is broken in the house, they feel responsible to fix it. Ownership is their posture.

But ownership is not the same as overthrow. Sons take responsibility for the vision of the father—they don't try to rewrite it. They don't undermine leadership, take liberties with the mission, or shift the culture to suit their preferences. True sons are not reformers in disguise trying to subvert the blueprint—they are loyal stewards who build faithfully on the foundation that was given to them.

Multiplying the Legacy of the Father's Vision

The highest honor of a spiritual son is not replacing the father—but multiplying his reach. Paul told Timothy, "The things that you have heard from me... commit these to faithful men who will be able to teach others also" (2 Timothy 2:2*). Paul wasn't trying to create carbon copies of himself—he was raising up sons who would carry the same fire, same doctrine, and same heart into every region they touched.

Apostolic building doesn't stop with one generation. The proof of sonship is not just obedience—it's reproduction. Elisha didn't just inherit Elijah's mantle; he expanded the prophetic legacy. Joshua didn't just serve Moses; he carried the people into the Promised Land. Jesus didn't just preach to the masses —He poured into twelve, and they turned the world upside down.

This is the difference between a servant and a son. A servant follows instructions. A son inherits a mission. The

* NKJV

apostolic father doesn't raise workers—he raises builders. Sons replicate what they've caught, and that legacy outlives the man who started it.

Sons Build What They've Caught—Not Just What They've Been Taught

There's a powerful truth that separates apostolic houses from religious institutions: what builds the house is not just information, but impartation. You can attend every training and memorize every policy, but if you don't catch the spirit of the house, you'll always serve as a hired hand instead of a son.

This is why proximity matters. You don't catch heart from a livestream. You catch heart in the hallway, the prayer meeting, the late-night cleanup crew, the awkward conversations, and the moments no one else sees. Sons don't serve for the platform —they serve to carry the weight. And in doing so, they receive what can never be taught—only caught.

Spiritual DNA is transferred through relational proximity. Sons serve close enough to see the weakness of their leader and still honor him. They don't get bitter with access—they grow in burden. They don't use familiarity as a weapon—they use it as a mirror to become more like Christ. That's what separates sons from spectators.

Faithfulness Precedes Fruitfulness

Jesus said, "If you have not been faithful in what is another man's, who will give you what is your own?" (Luke 16:12*). Before God ever gives you your own sphere of influence, He

---

* NKJV

watches how you serve under someone else's. If you're too big to follow, you're too small to lead.

Apostolic houses are training grounds. Not for ambition—but for faithfulness. Sons and daughters are tested in the unseen before they're trusted in the spotlight. They learn to steward vision, culture, and people with humility before they ever lead on their own. Why? Because the goal is not just to raise leaders—it's to raise pure ones.

The modern church often celebrates giftedness. But apostolic leaders prioritize character. Gifting might open doors, but only faithfulness keeps you standing when the weight of leadership comes. Sons grow into their calling by stewarding responsibility with excellence—even when it's not glamorous.

Serving Without Losing Sonship

One of the traps the enemy sets for emerging sons is to get them stuck in performance. If you only know how to be loved when you're serving, you're not a son—you're a slave with a spiritual mask.

You don't earn your place in the apostolic house by performance. You receive your place through alignment and relationship. Yes, you're called to work. Yes, you'll be stretched. But your identity as a son is secure even when you're benched, corrected, or hidden.

Sons who know they're loved serve differently. They don't grow resentful when they're not promoted. They don't question their worth when their role changes. They don't rebel when their season shifts. They serve from rest—not from striving. They obey because they love—not because they fear rejection.

The Fruit of Sonship Is Reproduction

Every father is looking for a son who can carry the legacy further. Every son should desire to multiply what he's been entrusted. That's the essence of the apostolic—sent ones, who carry something living and powerful from the house they were raised in.

If what you carry dies with you, you built wrong. Sons don't just build for today—they build for tomorrow. And as they grow in maturity, they become fathers to others. That's how the apostolic house increases: not through replacement, but reproduction.

Reproducing the house means reproducing the heart of the house. It means starting churches, ministries, and movements that sound and smell like the spiritual DNA of where they were birthed. It means planting with honor, sending with blessing, and expanding without losing the foundation.

The Mark of True Sons

True sons are not flashy. They're faithful. They don't need recognition to stay motivated. They don't need position to feel powerful. They carry the burden with their father, even when the load is heavy. And when their father can't carry it anymore —they lift his arms, like Aaron and Hur did for Moses.

True sons are not impressed by titles—they are hungry for impartation. They don't run to be seen—they run to serve. And as they do, they become part of something eternal—a house built not by men, but by God.

This is what the apostolic house needs. Not more volunteers. Not more opportunists. But sons—who build what they've caught. Who multiply what they've inherited. Who serve with fire and finish with fruit.

Discussion Questions

1. **From Duty to Devotion:** The chapter begins by saying, *"There is a vast difference between someone who is loyal out of duty and someone who is faithful out of love."* What motivates your service right now—duty, expectation, or love? How can you cultivate a heart that serves from sonship rather than from performance or pressure?

2. **Carrying, Not Controlling:** It says, *"Sons take ownership, not to control, but to carry."* How does this reshape the way you view leadership, authority, and responsibility in your house? What would it look like for you to carry more of the burden of the vision without trying to take over the mission?

3. **Reproducing the Heart of the House:** The chapter teaches that *"Reproducing the house means reproducing the heart of the house."* In what ways are you currently reproducing what you've caught—not just what you've been taught? How can you ensure that what you build, disciple, or lead reflects the same heart, culture, and DNA of the spiritual family that formed you?

CHAPTER 14

REPRODUCING THE CULTURE — FROM DISCIPLE TO LEADER

E very apostolic house rises or falls on culture. Strategies can change. Methods evolve. But the culture—the unseen values, behaviors, language, and atmosphere—must be preserved and reproduced if the house is to grow with integrity. Leaders are not just carriers of tasks; they are carriers of culture. And in apostolic houses, disciples must be trained not only to serve, but to steward what makes the house spiritually distinct.

Training Others in the Same Culture and Honor You've Received

Before someone becomes a leader, they must first become a disciple. But discipleship in the apostolic house isn't about information transfer. It's about transformation by impartation. It's one thing to know how things are done; it's another to know why they're done that way—and to do it with the same spirit.

Paul told Timothy, "You have carefully followed my doctrine, manner of life, purpose, faith, longsuffering, love, perseverance..." (2 Timothy 3:10*). Timothy didn't just follow Paul's sermons—he followed his lifestyle. He watched how Paul responded to adversity. He mirrored the way he treated people. He carried the tone of his teaching with the tenderness of his heart.

This is the assignment of every disciple who is being raised into leadership: to train others in the same spirit of honor, humility, and excellence they received. If you were discipled in a culture of bold faith, sacrificial service, and deep accountability, you must reproduce that same culture in those you lead.

And here's the key: you don't train others by mere repetition. You train them by modeling. People do what you do, not what you say. So if you were taught to greet your apostolic leader with respect, carry the house's language, and honor the altar with sobriety—then teach others by example. Let your consistency become the curriculum.

Raising Up Other Builders Without Losing the DNA

Multiplication without preservation is mutation. That's why apostolic leaders don't just raise up workers—they raise builders. Builders are those who know the blueprint, understand the weight, and steward both structure and spirit. They don't just execute tasks—they protect the house.

But how do you raise up other builders without losing what made the house special in the first place? By developing leaders who are sons, not employees with assignments. You raise up builders by instilling in them the spiritual DNA of the house. That includes:

---

* NKJV

- Language — They speak like the house. Not religious clichés, but language formed by revelation.
- Honor — They never dishonor leadership, the house, or each other.
- Spiritual posture — They're worshipers. They value prayer, fasting, the Word, and holiness.
- Relational culture — They're family, not just function. They protect unity and trust.

Builders must be formed with a deep understanding of what they're building. That's why delegation is not simply about who's available—it's about who is aligned. Don't put someone in charge of building if they don't love what's being built.

In apostolic houses, alignment is more important than availability. And culture is more important than convenience. You must be willing to slow down in multiplication so you don't accelerate mutation.

Multiplication Without Mutation

Jesus didn't send out the 12 until they had been with Him. They didn't just hear His teaching—they saw how He treated children, sinners, Pharisees, and the hurting. They caught His pace, His power, and His prayer life. That's why when they were sent, they didn't misrepresent Him. They carried His likeness.

In apostolic houses, leaders are often tempted to multiply teams, churches, ministries, or systems quickly. But speed without discipleship leads to distortion. You can end up with satellite ministries that no longer carry the culture—just the name.

How do you guard against mutation?

- Stay relational, not just organizational. The people you're raising must be in relationship with the house —not just compliance with a structure.
- Require proximity. Don't multiply what hasn't been discipled up close.
- Insist on heart checks. The moment someone stops honoring, you're not multiplying—you're fracturing.

You can only reproduce what you've embodied. You can only entrust the vision to those who've been formed by it.

From Disciple to Leader: The Maturity Test

Not every disciple is ready to lead. Leadership in the apostolic house is not a reward for talent—it is a responsibility entrusted to those who've been tested in culture. Every disciple must pass through several stages before they carry others:

1. Learning the Language — Does the disciple speak the heart of the house? Or do they speak out of offense, insecurity, or independence?
2. Walking in Honor — Do they consistently honor leaders, peers, and newcomers? Can they be corrected without pouting?
3. Embracing the Weight — Do they show up with spiritual and practical consistency? Do they feel responsible for the house's spiritual atmosphere?
4. Reproducing Others — Are they bringing others into the culture? Are they replicating maturity and joy, not just skill?
5. Being Sent, Not Just Stepping Out — True leadership begins with being sent. Those who self-promote will not preserve the house.

The goal of every apostolic leader is not just to find volunteers—it is to form vessels. You are not building a ministry team. You are building a spiritual family that reproduces the Kingdom with integrity.

Leading Without Losing Your Disciple's Heart

One of the final tests for any emerging leader is this: can you lead without losing your posture as a disciple? The moment a leader stops learning, stops submitting, or stops receiving correction, they begin to unravel the very culture they were formed by.

In apostolic houses, every leader remains under covering. That's not legalism—it's safety. You don't outgrow sonship. You grow in it.

You can carry great weight and still carry a teachable spirit. You can train others and still be trained. You can be trusted with much and still report with joy. This is the apostolic model —where leaders remain sons and daughters even as they lead teams, departments, or churches.

That's how the culture stays pure. That's how the house multiplies with the same fire. That's how generations are raised in alignment, not just excitement.

Be the Culture You Want to Multiply

In the end, the house doesn't grow because of how many seats are filled. It grows because of how many hearts are aligned. It grows because sons become leaders without losing the heart of a disciple. It grows because every multiplication is rooted in the original DNA—honor, worship, boldness, love, sacrifice, and truth.

If you want to lead in an apostolic house, don't just learn the structure—carry the spirit. Don't just execute tasks— preserve the atmosphere. Don't just show up on Sundays—live the culture every day.

Be the culture you want to multiply.

Discussion Questions

1. **Modeling the Culture You've Caught:** The chapter says, *"You don't train others by mere repetition. You train them by modeling. People do what you do, not what you say."* How does that challenge the way you currently lead, serve, or disciple others? What parts of your lifestyle, words, or attitude are already training those around you—intentionally or unintentionally?

2. **Multiplication Without Mutation:** It warns, *"Speed without discipleship leads to distortion."* In what areas of your ministry or leadership have you been tempted to multiply too quickly? What practical steps can you take to ensure that growth never outpaces discipleship, and that the house's spiritual DNA is preserved?

3. **Leading While Remaining a Disciple:** The chapter reminds us, *"You don't outgrow sonship. You grow in it."* What does that look like in your own journey? How can you stay teachable, humble, and submitted while still leading others? What disciplines or relationships help you remain anchored in the heart of a disciple?

CONCLUSION
BUILDING WHAT HEAVEN HAS BLUEPRINTED

There is a blueprint in Heaven. It's not the blueprint of man's ambition, religious systems, or the latest church-growth strategies. It's the eternal pattern of how God builds His house —a dwelling place for His glory, a family for His name, and a people through whom His Kingdom comes on Earth as it is in Heaven.

Apostolic leaders are not architects of their own imagination. They are stewards of divine design. They build what they've seen in the Spirit. Like Moses on Mount Sinai, they receive the pattern and return to the people with heaven's blueprint in their heart, ready to labor until what they've seen in prayer becomes tangible on Earth. But the apostolic house is not built by one man alone.

Apostles Build What God Has Shown—Not What People Prefer

Apostolic building will often offend the preferences of the flesh. It may seem slower than the demands of the impatient. It may resist the applause of the crowd. It may require structures, honor, submission, and spiritual formation that some consider outdated. But this is not a man-made movement—it's a God-ordained construction.

God never asked Moses, "What do the people want the tabernacle to look like?" He told Moses, "See that you make all things according to the pattern shown you on the mountain" (Hebrews 8:5*).

Likewise, apostles today are entrusted not with trends, but with templates from Heaven. They don't exist to entertain; they exist to establish. They don't conform to culture; they confront it. Their responsibility is not to gather crowds, but to raise sons and builders who carry the vision with holiness, clarity, and joy.

Disciples Help Birth, Protect, and Expand That Vision

No apostolic leader can build alone. In fact, God never intended for apostles to function apart from family. That's where you come in.

You were not saved just to attend a church. You were saved to be joined to a family, called to a house, and assigned to a vision. Apostolic discipleship is not passive. It requires your yes. It requires your alignment. It requires your maturity and your servanthood.

You are part of something bigger than yourself. And your role matters.

---

* NKJV

You help birth the vision by being present in the early days —when it's fragile, when it's costly, when it's not fully formed yet. You protect the vision by refusing offense, resisting division, and honoring the leader God has appointed over the house. You expand the vision by serving with excellence, raising others, and stepping into leadership as maturity allows.

This is how apostolic houses become movements—not through one man's gifting, but through a company of sons and daughters who've caught the spirit and joined the work.

Your Role Matters. Find It. Own It. Build It with All Your Heart.

This book has not been about theory. It's been a call to build. And now, as you turn this final page, you must ask yourself: Where is my place in this house?

Are you a disciple just beginning the journey? Are you a servant stewarding small things with faithfulness? Are you a leader raising others in the same spirit you've received? Are you a son or daughter carrying the weight of the house with joy? Whatever your role, know this: you are vital. You are seen. You are called.

Apostolic houses are built by disciples who become sons, servants who become leaders, and people who lay down preference for the sake of presence and purpose. That's you. You are part of God's building project on the Earth.

So build with all your heart. Build with joy. Build with the blueprints of Heaven burned into your spirit. And never forget —what you're part of is bigger than you. But it cannot be built without you.

Final Charge: Built Together

As Paul wrote in Ephesians 2:19–22:

"Now, therefore, you are no longer strangers and foreigners, but fellow citizens with the saints and members of the household of God, having been built on the foundation of the apostles and prophets, Jesus Christ Himself being the chief cornerstone, in whom the whole building, being fitted together, grows into a holy temple in the Lord, in whom you also are being built together for a dwelling place of God in the Spirit." NKJV

That's the vision. Not just one apostle building alone—but a people being built together. Let the Holy Spirit place you where you belong. Let your leader shape you with wisdom and love. Let your life become a stone in the wall, a beam in the ceiling, a stake in the foundation of something eternal. You were made for this.

ABOUT THE AUTHOR

Tom Cornell is the Senior Leader of SOZO Church in Washington state, founder of Walk in the Light International and SOZO Network. Tom is married to his beautiful wife Katy and lives in the Puget Sound area with her and their three kids. He has been in ministry pastoring and teaching the body of Christ since 2008.

He has a passion to see the body of Christ moving from people with an orphan mindset to that of sonship; equipping the body to do the work of Jesus resulting in seeing the Kingdom of God manifested here on earth.